EFFECTIVE ACADEMIC WRITING 3

THE ESSAY

JASON DAVIS
Bronx Community College,
City University of New York

RHONDA LISS
Bronx Community College,
City University of New York

OXFORD
UNIVERSITY PRESS

OXFORD
UNIVERSITY PRESS

198 Madison Avenue
New York, NY 10016 USA

Great Clarendon Street, Oxford OX2 6DP UK

Oxford University Press is a department of the University of Oxford.
It furthers the University's objective of excellence in research, scholarship,
and education by publishing worldwide in

Oxford New York

Auckland Cape Town Dar es Salaam Hong Kong Karachi
Kuala Lumpur Madrid Melbourne Mexico City Nairobi
New Delhi Shanghai Taipei Toronto

With offices in

Argentina Austria Brazil Chile Czech Republic France Greece
Guatemala Hungary Italy Japan Poland Portugal Singapore
South Korea Switzerland Thailand Turkey Ukraine Vietnam

OXFORD and OXFORD ENGLISH are registered trademarks of
Oxford University Press

© Oxford University Press 2006

Database right Oxford University Press (maker)

Library of Congress Cataloging-in-Publication Data

Davis, Jason.
    Effective academic writing 3 : the essay / Jason Davis, Rhonda Liss.
        p. cm.
    ISBN 978-0-19-43092924-0 (student book)
    ISBN 978-0-19-430884-7 (answer key)
    1. English language—Rhetoric—Problems, exercises, etc. 2. Essay—
Authorship—Problems, exercises, etc. 3. Report writing—Problems, exercises,
etc. I. Title: Effective academic writing two. II. Liss, Rhonda, III. Title.

PE1471.S28 2006
808'.042—dc22   2005030686

Executive Publisher: Janet Aitchison
Senior Acquisitions Editor: Pietro Alongi
Associate Editor: Scott Allan Wallick
Art Director: Maj-Britt Hagsted
Art Editor: Robin Fadool
Production Manager: Shanta Persaud
Production Controller: Eve Wong

ISBN 978-0-19-430924-0 (STUDENT BOOK)
ISBN 978-0-19-430884-7 (ANSWER KEY)

Printed in Hong Kong

10 9 8 7 6 5 4

ACKNOWLEDGMENTS

Cover art:
Richard Diebenkorn
Ocean Park #122; 1980
oil and charcoal on canvas; 100 in. x 80 5/8 in. (254 cm x204.79 cm)
San Francisco Museum of Modern Art
Charles H. Land Familiar Foundation Fund purchase
© Estate of Richard Diebenkorn

Illustration:
The New Yorker / Mike Twohy, 62; Jon Keegan, 96.

We would like to thank the following for their permission to reproduce photographs:
Masterfile: Horst Herget, 2; Photo Edit Inc.: David Young-Wolff, 2; Blend
Images/Punch Stock: 2; Top: Photo Edit Inc.: Gary Conner, 32; Bottom: Photo
Edit Inc.: Gary Conner, 32; National Archives/Time Life Pictures/Getty Images:
156; George Eastman House/Getty Images: Lewis W. Hine, 156; Time & Life
Pictures/Getty Images: Margaret Bourke-White, 162; Pix Inc./Time & Life
Pictures/Getty Images: Alfred Eisenstaedt, 162; Masterfile: Peter Christopher,
184; Brand X/Punch Stock: 184.

Acknowledgements

We would first like to thank our editorial team, Kenna Bourke and Scott Allan Wallick, for their insight and expertise. We are ever indebted to Kathleen Smith for acting as the perfect springboard for our ideas and to Pietro Alongi for his positive energy, enthusiasm, and dedication. We want to extend our thanks to the following reviewers for their contribution to the project: Sharon Allerson, East LA Community College; Frank Cronin, Austin Community College; Kieran Hilu, Virginia Tech; Peter Hoffman, LaGuardia Community College; Carla Nyssen, California State University Long Beach; Adrianne Ochoa; Mary O'Neill, North Virginia Community College; Maria Salinas, Del Mar College. We also want to gratefully acknowledge the work of Susan Kesner Bland.

Our thanks also go to Robert Cohen for getting us involved in this project, and to Fatiha Makloufi and Kim Sanabria for their continued encouragement. The warm support of the faculty and staff of the CUNY Language Immersion Program, especially Lee Spencer, was greatly appreciated. We are very grateful to our students whose struggles with the English language were the inspiration and backbone of activities in this book. Our students' amazing stories and startling creativity enhanced our own journey.

Thank you, Reid Strieby, for your constructive criticism, enduring support, patience, and wonderful home cooked meals—regardless of the hour. We look forward to renewing our relationships with our friends and family members, who remained enthusiastic throughout the writing of this book and who almost never complained when we couldn't see them. Finally, we would like to thank each other for always keeping the goal in sight, our energy alive, and our humor intact.

J.D. and R.L.

Contents

Unit 5: Classification Essays

Unit 6: Reaction Essays

Appendices

Introduction

Effective Academic Writing is a three-book series intended to usher students into the world of academic writing. The goal of the series is to provide students and their teachers with a practical and efficient approach to acquiring the skills, strategies, and knowledge that are necessary for succeeding in content coursework. A parallel goal is to provide opportunities for students to explore their opinions, discuss their ideas, and share their experiences through written communication. By guiding developing writers through the experience of composing various types of essays, we hope to provide students with the tools and the confidence necessary for college success.

The Essay

Book 3 of *Effective Academic Writing, The Essay,* introduces students at the high intermediate to low advanced level to five-paragraph essays. The first unit provides a thorough review of short essay structure and addresses issues of coherence and unity. Each of the following five units then addresses a particular rhetorical mode and provides user-friendly guidance to mastering the form. The book also offers numerous opportunities for practicing relevant grammar points. All grammar presentations and practice are correlated to *Grammar Sense 3*. Book 3 contains several features designed to support students in developing the skills that they need for college writing:

- Each unit contains an authentic text to provide ideas and context for the assignment.
- At strategic points in the unit, students read and analyze authentic student essays to see how other students have written on the same or similar topics.
- Each unit contains vocabulary and brainstorming activities which help students generate the language and concepts needed for their essays.
- Each unit contains concise and effective language presentations designed to develop students' understanding of rhetorical modes and to improve their grammatical accuracy.
- Each unit offers useful writing outlines so that students can structure their writing and internalize the practice.
- Each unit offers collaborative learning activities allowing students to work together and share ideas.
- At relevant points in the unit, editing exercises and editing checklists are provided so that students can refine their writing.
- Timed writing activities come at the close of each unit to prepare students for in-class writing.
- A series of learner-friendly appendices are provided at the back of the book to encourage student independence. A glossary of common grammar terms for student reference is included.

Unit Organization

Each unit introduces a theme and a writing task and then guides the writer through a five-part process of gathering ideas, organizing an outline, drafting, revising, and editing. As students write, they practice specific skills and put language knowledge to work to produce an essay that follows academic conventions. The rhetorical and language-related goals of the unit are identified on the opener page.

Part 1

Part 1 opens with an image to spark interest as students begin thinking about the topic. This is followed by a short authentic text. Students answer questions about the passage that will help them connect the writer's ideas to their own knowledge and experience. They then move on to a free-writing activity, an unstructured writing task in which they can explore the topic without worrying about organization or grammar.

Part 2

In Part 2 students are introduced to a specific rhetorical mode. They begin by brainstorming ideas and vocabulary that they will use to write their essay. They then learn about rhetorical organizational features and read and analyze a student essay. Finally, students produce an outline for the essay they will write later in the unit.

Part 3

In Part 3 students develop the ideas from their outline and produce a first draft. This part opens with a second student essay for students to analyze. As they answer questions about the second student model, students review the organizational features learned in Part 2. They are then introduced to specific, level-appropriate language points that will help students shape and structure their writing. Students now write their first draft and, using a peer-review checklist, check each other's writing for organization and clarity of ideas.

Part 4

In Part 4 students edit their writing and produce a final draft. This part focuses on particular grammar trouble spots relevant to the theme and the rhetorical style presented in the unit. Following the concise language presentation, students complete practice exercises to help them develop their grammar skills and build confidence. The last exercise always focuses on accuracy and involves editing a piece of writing. Students then move on to editing their own writing, and produce a final draft.

Part 5

The final part of the unit is titled "Putting It All Together." This is the summary of the other parts of the unit. Through a series of skill exercises, students review the points covered in Parts 1–4. They are then given the opportunity to write a timed essay using a similar rhetorical focus, but on a different topic. Guidelines for using their time efficiently are suggested. This part also provides students with a comprehensive checklist to review what they have written. The unit closes with suggested tasks for future writing that can be used for more practice.

Unit 1

The Five-Paragraph Essay

Unit Goals

Rhetorical focus:
- structure of the five-paragraph essay
- coherence and unity in paragraphs and essays

Language focus:
- main and dependent clauses
- run-on sentences and fragments
- verb tense consistency

| Exercise 1 | **Thinking about the topic** |

Discuss the questions with a partner.

- What types of writing are the students in the pictures practicing?
- Which of these types of writing have you experienced?
- Where and when do you like to write?
- What are the different kinds of writing you do?

Rhetorical Focus

Review of Short Essay Structure

A short essay has three basic parts: an introduction, one or two body paragraphs, and a conclusion. Each part is a separate paragraph. The first sentence of each paragraph is indented.

- The introduction is the first paragraph of the essay. It contains the thesis of the essay, which states what the entire essay is about.

- The body paragraphs develop the idea presented in the introduction. Each body paragraph has a topic sentence and details that support the thesis in the introduction. The topic sentence of a body paragraph also states what that body paragraph is about.

- The conclusion is the last paragraph. It brings the essay to a close.

Identifying the elements of a short essay

A. **Read the short essay about becoming an academic writer. Then label the parts of the essay. Use the words in the box.**

a. introduction	b. body paragraph	c. conclusion

Becoming an Academic Writer

1. ____ →

Learning how to write an academic essay is essential for students who are planning to attend college. Most professors require critiques of books and films, research papers, and formal reports related to the content of their courses. When I first started college, I was excited about facing these challenges and pursuing my major, media and communications. I was determined to improve my writing. To achieve this goal, I focused on three points: the content of an essay, correct grammar, and advanced level vocabulary.

2. ____ →

As soon as I started to write for college, I realized that college writing was different from the writing I was used to doing. In high school, most of my writing dealt with my personal experiences. I wrote mainly about my family, childhood, and friends. In contrast, college writing focused on a variety of issues that I was unfamiliar with, such as reacting to a piece of literature or writing about the community. Therefore, the most important thing for me was to understand the assigned topic before attempting my first draft. Moreover, I realized that I had to improve my understanding of grammar in order to write for college. Consequently, I made grammar my second priority. I reviewed the basic grammatical structures such as subjects and verbs, and checked all my work for verb tense consistency and punctuation. Lastly, because I was accustomed to writing letters and informal essays, I usually wrote the way I spoke with my family and friends. I soon realized that academic writing required a much more sophisticated vocabulary. Thus, I bought a new dictionary and thesaurus to help expand my vocabulary.

3. ____ →

Academic writing requires critical thinking skills, an understanding of the topic, high level vocabulary, and correct grammar. Having these skills is empowering since it has made me a better communicator and student. I have come a long way since I started college, and I am now proud of the writing that I produce.

B. Answer the questions about the short essay on page 3. Then compare your answers with a partner.

1. Underline the thesis statement in the introduction. Why is it the thesis of the essay? _____

   _____

   _____

2. Underline the topic sentence of the body paragraph. What makes it the topic sentence? _____

   _____

   _____

3. In what way do the details in the body paragraph support the topic sentence? _____

   _____

4. In what way does the conclusion complete the essay? _____

   _____

   _____

Rhetorical Focus

The Short Essay and the Five-Paragraph Essay

You may have written short essays, but as you progress in your academic studies, your teachers will expect five-paragraph essays that are longer and more sophisticated. These essays have greater elaboration, which may include examples, statistics, questions, definitions, quotations, and anecdotes. They are more analytical in nature.

Like a short essay, a five-paragraph essay has three basic parts: an introduction, a body, and a conclusion. However, unlike a short essay that may contain only one or two body paragraphs, a five-paragraph essay has three body paragraphs. Each body paragraph contains a topic sentence that supports the thesis statement.

Reading a five-paragraph essay

A. **Read the five-paragraph essay below about becoming an academic writer. Compare it to the short essay on page 3. How are the two essays different?**

Becoming an Academic Writer

Learning how to write an academic essay is essential for students who are planning to attend college. Most professors require critiques of books and films, research papers, and formal reports related to the content of their courses. When I first started college, I was excited about facing these challenges and pursuing my major, media and communications. I was determined to improve my writing. To achieve this goal, I focused on three points: the content of an essay, correct grammar, and advanced level vocabulary.

> introduction

As soon as I started to write for college, I realized that college writing was different from the writing I was used to doing. In high school, most of my writing dealt with my personal experiences. I wrote mainly about my family, childhood, and friends. In contrast, college writing focused on a variety of issues that I was unfamiliar with, such as reacting to a piece of literature or writing about the community. Therefore, the most important thing for me was to understand the assigned topic before attempting my first draft. In some cases, I would have to read and do research to build a foundation. I wanted to include examples, statistics, and direct quotations whenever possible to support my opinions. By giving specific examples, I realized that my essays became more detailed, easier to read, and much more interesting. However, grammatical problems in my writing were still an issue.

> body paragraph 1

I realized that I had to improve my understanding of grammar in order to write for college. Before I came to college, grammar was not my strong point. For example, I often created run-on sentences

> body paragraph 2

or sentence fragments. I was more concerned with what I wanted to say than with how it was said. In fact, my professors would not accept this type of writing and made me revise many times. Consequently, I made grammar my second priority. I reviewed the basic grammatical structures such as subjects and verbs and checked all my work for verb tense consistency and punctuation. As a result, my sentences became more complex because I included transitional words, gerunds, and embedded clauses. The more I wrote, the more my writing improved.

Furthermore, because I was accustomed to writing letters and informal essays, I usually wrote the way I spoke with my family and friends. It was quite common for me to include slang and abbreviated terms, which were appropriate in social contexts but were unacceptable in formal essays. I soon realized that academic writing required a much more sophisticated vocabulary. Not surprisingly, improving my vocabulary became my third and final goal. Thus, I bought a new dictionary and thesaurus to help expand my knowledge. I became more aware of how often I repeated the same words and phrases throughout my essay. I often searched for synonyms to replace words that I thought were too simple for a college essay. I also focused more on the rules of spelling and corrected any errors I found before submitting my assignment to the instructor.

Academic writing requires critical thinking skills, an understanding of the topic, high level vocabulary, and correct grammar. Having these skills is empowering since it has made me a better communicator and student. I have come a long way since I started college, and I am now proud of the writing that I produce.

body paragraph 3

conclusion

B. Answer the questions below. Then compare your answers with a partner.

1. Underline the thesis statement in the introduction. Is it different from the thesis of the short essay on page 3? _____

2. Underline the topic sentences of the body paragraphs. How do the topic sentences relate to the thesis statement? _____

   _____

   _____

3. How do the three body paragraphs of the five-paragraph essay expand on the information provided in the single body paragraph of the short essay?

   _____

   _____

   _____

4. Is the conclusion different from that of the short essay on page 3? _____

> **In Part 2 you will . . .**
> • learn more about five-paragraph essay organization.

PART 2

Developing the Five-Paragraph Essay

Rhetorical Focus

The Introduction

An introduction to a five-paragraph essay must have a hook, background information, and a thesis statement.

Hook

A hook is a statement that begins the introduction. It includes one or two interesting sentences that engage the readers' attention and stimulate their curiosity. The sentences below provide the hook for an essay about a wedding celebration.

> We all dream about our wedding celebration, but when it happens, we do not know what to expect.

Background Information

Background information in most cases follows the hook. The background information contains a general statement or statements that give a broader picture of the subject matter to be discussed. The sentences below provide the context (situation) for the essay on a wedding celebration.

> I met my husband on a student trip to Honduras. After four years of letter writing and visits, we finally announced our engagement and planned for the event.

Thesis Statements

A thesis statement usually comes at the end of the introduction. It summarizes what the entire essay is about. It contains the topic and the controlling idea for the whole essay. The topic is the theme or subject matter of the essay. The controlling idea defines the purpose of the essay and sets its direction.

topic	controlling idea

My wedding day <u>was the most thrilling day of my life</u>.

Examining an introduction

**Read this introduction to an essay then answer the questions below.
Compare your answers with a partner.**

One of the Best Moments of My Life

It was a sunny day in the summer of 1998 when my family moved out of the city to the suburbs. I did not like leaving because I would lose my friends and the places where I had had so much fun. It was very sad for me to see my friends standing in front of the old house as we said our last goodbyes. Little did I know that this move would turn out to be one of the best moments of my life.

---

1. Circle and label the hook.

2. Underline the background information.

3. Underline the thesis statement.

4. Write the topic of the thesis statement. _____

5. Write the controlling idea of the thesis statement. _____

_____

Rhetorical Focus

Body Paragraphs

The three body paragraphs of a five-paragraph essay contain the supporting details of the essay.

- The topic sentence clearly states the content of each paragraph. It supports and expands on an aspect of the topic and controlling idea of the thesis statement. The topic sentence is often the first sentence of a body paragraph.

- Each body paragraph must develop a point presented in the topic statement. All the supporting details in a body paragraph must clearly relate to each other. They can be description, definitions, examples, anecdotes, statistics, or quotations. Quotations may come from a published work or from a personal interview.

- The concluding sentence may either bring the idea of the paragraph to a close or suggest the content of the next paragraph.

Examining body paragraphs

Examine the body paragraphs of the five-paragraph essay on pages 5–6. Then answer the questions below. Compare your answers with a partner.

Body Paragraph 1

1. Underline the topic sentence. Then write the topic sentence in your own words. _____

   _____

2. What supporting details are provided? How do they support the topic sentence? _____

   _____

3. The concluding sentence

   a. brings the idea of the paragraph to a close.

   b. suggests the content of the next paragraph.

Body Paragraph 2

1. Underline the topic sentence. Then write the topic sentence in your own words. _____

   _____

2. What supporting details are provided? How do they support the topic sentence? _____

   _____

3. The concluding sentence

   a. brings the idea of the paragraph to a close.

   b. suggests the content of the next paragraph.

Body Paragraph 3

1. Underline the topic sentence. Then write the topic sentence in your own words. _____

   _____

2. What details are provided? How do they support the topic sentence? _____

   _____

3. The concluding sentence

   a. brings the idea of the paragraph to a close.

   b. suggests the content of the next paragraph.

Rhetorical Focus

The Conclusion

All five-paragraph essays end with a conclusion that brings the essay to a close.

- The conclusion is usually two to four sentences in length.
- It restates the thesis of the introduction in different words. This restatement connects the conclusion to the introduction.
- It may give advice or a warning.
- It may make a prediction or ask a question.
- It can provide new insights and discoveries that the writer has gained through writing the essay.

Exercise 3   Examining a conclusion

Reread the conclusion of "Becoming an Academic Writer." Then answer the questions below.

> Academic writing requires critical thinking skills, an understanding of the topic, high level vocabulary, and correct grammar. Having these skills is empowering since it has made me a better communicator and student. I have come a long way since I started college, and I am now proud of the writing that I produce.

1. How many sentences appear in the conclusion?_____

2. Underline the sentence in the conclusion that restates the thesis in the introduction.

3. The conclusion ends with
   a. some advice.
   b. a prediction.
   c. a warning.
   d. an insight.

In Part 3 you will . . .
- learn about unity and coherence.

PART 3

Unity and Coherence

Rhetorical Focus

Unity

Effective writing must have unity. Unity occurs when all the ideas in a paragraph or an essay support each other.

Unity Within a Paragraph

A paragraph has unity when all the sentences support the topic sentence, the main idea of the paragraph. Without unity, the paragraph loses focus. The topic sentence of the paragraph should focus on **one** topic and controlling idea. The supporting details of the paragraph must support the topic and controlling idea of the topic sentence. If they do not, they will be irrelevant and destroy the unity of the essay.

The paragraph below contains sentences that do not support the topic and controlling idea expressed in the topic sentence. These irrelevant sentences have been crossed out in order to preserve unity.

Jay Gatsby was my favorite character in the novel *The Great Gatsby* by F. Scott Fitzgerald. ~~This is a classic American novel.~~ One of the qualities I valued most about him was his generosity and loyalty to his friends and neighbors. For example, he gave many extravagant parties and never thought about the cost. He invited anyone he knew and liked regardless of their social status. ~~His large home was situated on the water on Long Island.~~ In fact, he befriended a struggling young man and offered to help him earn more money. ~~This book is required reading in many college courses because it reveals the lifestyles of the 1920s.~~ Although this young man remained faithful to Gatsby, others took advantage of his good nature.

Exercise 1 | **Editing for unity**

Read the two paragraphs. Draw a line through the sentences that are irrelevant. The first one is done for you. There are six more.

Having my friends and family together at my wedding was an amazing experience. I had not seen some of my uncles, cousins, and aunts for many years. ~~My cousin Tom lives in London, where he works as an engineer.~~ Both my mother and father were born in different countries, so my relatives are scattered all over the world. I really like traveling and have been to Europe and Asia. Although we try to get together for important occasions, this was the first time everyone could attend. Most importantly, my good friends had never met my relatives. Developing good friendships takes a lot of work. Watching them all dancing, laughing, and having a wonderful time will stay in my memory forever.

The band we hired played music that the guests loved and we danced for hours. My original guest list had over 200 people, but I had to cut it down to 150. It was difficult finding a group that could play all the diverse styles that I wanted at the wedding. Most bands specialize in one or two different kinds of music. However, these musicians really knew all types of music—from 1940s jazz and swing, to salsa, merengue, and even hip-hop. My brother was once in a rock and roll band. In short, there was music to suit everyone's tastes. I loved the singer's dress. It was incredible. Even my grandparents danced all night.

Rhetorical Focus

Unity Within an Essay

An essay has unity when all the body paragraphs contain a topic sentence and supporting sentences that reinforce the thesis of the essay. Without unity, the essay loses focus and goes off the topic.

In the example below, topic sentences 1 and 2 both support the thesis statement. However, notice how topic sentence 3 goes off the topic.

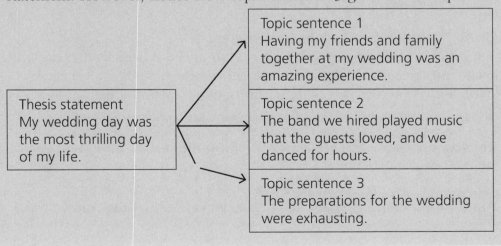

Thesis statement
My wedding day was the most thrilling day of my life.

Topic sentence 1
Having my friends and family together at my wedding was an amazing experience.

Topic sentence 2
The band we hired played music that the guests loved, and we danced for hours.

Topic sentence 3
The preparations for the wedding were exhausting.

Recognizing unity within an essay

Read the following thesis statements. Put a check (✔) next to each topic sentence that supports the thesis statement.

1. **Thesis:** After two years of job hunting, I have finally found the perfect job for me.

Topic sentences:

_____ a. I am enthusiastic about the challenges that I confront at work every day.

_____ b. Last year I almost got a good job.

_____ c. I am making more money than I have ever made, and have so many benefits.

_____ d. My boss is very supportive and is helping me to succeed.

_____ e. I did not like the job I had before.

2. **Thesis:** Skiing is a great sport, but it is not for everyone.

Topic sentences:

_____ a. Not everyone has the ability to ski well.

_____ b. Becoming a good skier means taking certain risks that some people are afraid to take.

_____ c. Skiing is more difficult than ice skating.

_____ d. A day on the slopes is not always affordable for everyone.

_____ e. Skiing down the highest slope can be dangerous.

Rhetorical Focus

Coherence

Coherence in a paragraph means that all the ideas fit together in a logical flow. In a coherent paragraph, the relationship between ideas is clear, and one idea connects logically to the next. Coherence can be achieved by using transition expressions, logical order, pronouns, and parallel forms.

Using Transition Expressions for Coherence

Transition expressions show how one sentence relates to another and create a logical flow. The example below shows how the transition expression *however* serves to set up two contrasting ideas.

She likes to read novels. **However**, she does not enjoy biographies.

Transition expressions are separated from the rest of the sentence by commas.

I enjoy writing in my journal. **However**, I do not like writing letters.
I enjoy writing in my journal. I do not like writing letters, **however**.

Transition expressions can be used with a semicolon and a comma to form a compound sentence.

His first novel was not a success; **however**, his second work became a bestseller.

Below is a list of some transition words and their use.

Use	Transition Expressions
Example	*for instance, to demonstrate, for example, in some cases*
Additional idea	*moreover, furthermore, in addition*
Contrast	*however, in contrast, on the contrary, nevertheless, nonetheless*
Cause	*as a result, therefore, thus, consequently*
Emphasis	*indeed, in fact, obviously*

Exercise 3   Identifying coherence

One sentence is missing from each short paragraph below. Choose the sentence that best completes the paragraph.

1. In many ways the invention of e-mail and computers has motivated many young people to take up letter writing. E-mail makes it fun and easy to get in touch with faraway friends. _____ For these reasons fewer people are sending letters through the mail.

    a. I bought a new computer last week.

    b. Furthermore, e-mail is convenient and essentially free.

2. Books on tape have become very popular in our fast-paced society. One of the reasons is that people do not have the time to sit still and read. _____ Some listen while jogging outdoors or exercising in the gym. Therefore, a book on tape makes for a great gift idea for the active book lover.

    a. Stephen King's latest book is available in this format.

    b. In fact, many people listen to these tapes while driving to and from work.

3. *Don Quixote de la Mancha* is an epic novel written in the 1600s by Miguel de Cervantes. This is the story of a man who read so many books on chivalry and knighthood that he went crazy. _____ Together they had many adventures always searching for truth and beauty and upholding the highest ideals.

    a. He traveled the world as a ridiculous knight along with his friend Sancho Panza.

    b. Don Quixote came from a small town in Spain called La Mancha.

Using transition expressions in sentences

Combine the following sentences to create coherence by using transition expressions from the box.

> in contrast   nevertheless   previously   ~~therefore~~   for example   moreover

1. I want to study in Italy for a year to learn about art. I enrolled in Italian classes.

   <u>I want to study in Italy for a year to learn about art. Therefore, I enrolled</u>
   <u>in Italian classes.</u>

2. Learning a foreign language takes a lot of patience and effort. It helps to have a good ear.

   _____

   _____

3. The college student was told to revise her essay a third time. She has still made great progress with her writing skills.

   _____

   _____

4. John Steinbeck, a famous American author, wrote many books concerning the human condition. His novel *The Grapes of Wrath* dealt with the problems of the Great Depression.

   _____

   _____

5. Academic writing requires a knowledge of standard grammar, sophisticated vocabulary, and proper organization. E-mail messages use abbreviations, symbols, and slang.

   _____

   _____

6. Nowadays research is often done on the Internet. Important information was stored on special film called microfiche.

   _____

   _____

Rhetorical Focus

Ordering Ideas for Coherence

One way to achieve coherence in an essay is to arrange ideas in a logical order, such as chronological order or order of importance.

- When arranging ideas in chronological order, use language such as *in the beginning, next, then, first, second,* or *finally.*

   First, I went to the bank. **Next**, I visited my mother in the hospital.

- When arranging ideas in order of importance, you order items from the most important to the least important or vice versa. Use language such as *the most/least important thing, the next priority/most important thing,* or *the third/final priority/goal.*

   The most important thing for me was to understand the assigned topic before attempting my first draft.

Exercise 5 **Ordering ideas in a paragraph**

A. **Use the list of ideas to write a short paragraph. Arrange your ideas in chronological order. Use language from the Rhetorical Focus box above. The first sentence has been done for you.**

- boil water
- add rice
- cook for about twenty minutes

If you want to make rice, first boil some water.

_____

_____

_____

B. **Use the list of ideas to write a short paragraph. Arrange your ideas in order of importance. Use language from the Rhetorical Focus box above.**

- practice speaking Spanish with friends
- take a class in Spanish
- visit a Spanish-speaking country

_____

_____

_____

_____

Rhetorical Focus

Using Pronoun Reference for Coherence

A pronoun is a word that can replace a noun. *I, you, he, it, this, that, those,* and *these* are some examples of pronouns. Pronouns can be used to create coherence in an essay.

What is <u>revision</u> and why is **it** necessary?

Pronouns can also replace whole phrases or ideas.

<u>I left my expensive dictionary in the library.</u> I do not know how I did **that**.

⚠ Pronouns must agree in number and gender with the noun they refer to.
 I have a younger <u>brother</u>. **He** is a lawyer.
 I have a younger brother. She is a lawyer. (INCORRECT)

Exercise 6   **Identifying pronoun reference**

Read the paragraph. Choose the correct pronoun to complete each sentence.

On Sunday afternoon, my mother and I went to visit my uncle. I told my mother that I was looking forward to seeing (him / her) again.
                                                                 1.
(She / He) was delighted to hear (this / I) . Unfortunately, my sister
  2.   3.
Diana and my father were unable to attend because (they / he) had to
                                                              4.
work that weekend. My mother and I drove to my uncle's house. When
(we / I) arrived, my uncle and his wife greeted (us / we) at the door.
  5.   6.
(They / She) were very excited to see (us / it) .
  7.   8.

Rhetorical Focus

Using Parallel Forms for Coherence

Another strategy to achieve coherence is by using parallel forms.
This means that all items in a list have the same grammatical form.

I like **playing** tennis, **swimming**, and **dancing**.
I like playing tennis, swimming, and to dance. (INCORRECT)

She **cooked** dinner, **set** the table, and **arranged** the flowers.
She cooked dinner, set the table, and the flowers were arranged. (INCORRECT)

Exercise 7 | **Practicing with parallel forms**

Rewrite the following sentences to correct the non-parallel forms.

1. At the age of twenty, I started to write plays, taking acting lessons, and produce shows.

   At the age of twenty, I started to write plays, take acting lessons, and
   produce shows.

2. As a teenager, I reported on school events, editing articles for the high school newspaper, and published some of my stories.

   _____

   _____

3. Some of the rewards of being an author are learn about historical events, researching the lives of famous people, and discovering facts about yourself.

   _____

   _____

4. Attending workshops on writing have taught me how to receive criticism, became a more focused writer, and take more risks.

   _____

   _____

In Part 4 you will . . .

- learn about main and dependent clauses.
- learn how to correct run-ons and sentence fragments.
- learn about verb tense consistency.

PART 4

Editing Your Writing

Language Focus

Clauses

Every clause in English must have a subject and a verb. There are two types of clauses: main clauses and dependent clauses.

Main Clauses

A main clause contains a complete idea and can stand alone as a sentence.

I read my speech at graduation.

Dependent Clauses

A dependent clause does not contain a complete idea and cannot stand alone as a complete sentence. A dependent clause often starts with a subordinating conjunction such as *after, before, although, because, since, when,* or *while*. A dependent clause can be attached to a main clause in order to form a complex sentence. A dependent clause can come before or after the main clause, but the punctuation is different.

• When the dependent clause begins the sentence, place a comma after it.

dependent clause	main clause

When I read my speech at graduation, all my friends and family were amazed.

• When the independent clause comes at the end of the sentence, omit the comma.

main clause	dependent clause

All my friends and family were amazed **when I read my speech at graduation.**

Exercise 1	**Identifying main and dependent clauses**

Underline the dependent clause and circle the main clause in each sentence. Add punctuation if necessary.

1. When I came into the auditorium, the room was empty.
2. I felt very confident because I had spent a long time practicing.
3. Since it was my graduation I bought a beautiful new outfit.
4. Although the ceremony was very long nobody was bored.
5. We went out for a fancy meal after the ceremony ended.
6. My family took a lot of photographs which I still enjoy looking at.

Language Focus

Run-on Sentences

Run-on sentences are incorrect sentences. Run-on sentence errors occur when two main clauses occur together with no connector or punctuation between them:

Langston Hughes was an important poet of the Harlem Renaissance he also wrote very fine short stories. (INCORRECT)

Run-on sentence errors can also occur when two main clauses are separated by a comma.

Langston Hughes was an important poet of the Harlem Renaissance, he also wrote very fine short stories. (INCORRECT)

A run-on sentence can be corrected in several ways.

- You can change one of the main clauses to a dependent clause by adding a subordinating conjunction such as *because, when, before,* or *although.*

  Although Langston Hughes was an important poet of the Harlem Renaissance, he also wrote very fine short stories.

- You can use a coordinating conjunctions such as *and, but, yet, so, or,* or *for* to connect the two clauses and to form a compound sentence. Use a comma before the coordinating conjunction.

  Langston Hughes was an important poet of the Harlem Renaissance, **but** he also wrote very fine short stories.

- You can also use punctuation to correct a run-on sentence. Use a period between two main clauses that contain two separate and distinct ideas. Use a semicolon between the clauses that are very close in meaning.

  Langston Hughes was an important poet of the Harlem Renaissance; his first poem was one of his most famous.

| Exercise 2 | **Identifying run-on sentences** |

Write *RO* next to the run-on sentences and *C* next to the correct sentences.

_____ 1. My family and I came from Vietnam I was 16 years old.

_____ 2. I came to the United States I did not know English.

_____ 3. Because I did not know English, I was worried about my future.

_____ 4. People are very busy working they do not have time to study.

_____ 5. Since I now know both languages, I can help my parents.

Correcting run-on sentences with coordinating conjunctions

Use a coordinating conjunction from the box to correct each run-on sentence. You may use each coordinating conjunction more than once.

and	but	so	or	yet	for

1. The great American author Mark Twain traveled a lot, he still made time for his daughter.

   The great American author Mark Twain traveled a lot, but he still made time for his daughter.

2. The nineteenth-century British novelist Charlotte Bronte wrote *Jane Eyre*, her younger sister Emily was the author of the classic *Wuthering Heights*.

   _____

   _____

3. Upton Sinclair was concerned about social and political problems of his times, he wrote *The Jungle* exposing the unsanitary conditions of the meatpacking industry.

   _____

   _____

4. Jane Austen's original version of *Pride and Prejudice* was written when she was only twenty years old, it was not published for almost two decades.

   _____

   _____

5. The anthropologist Margaret Mead went to Samoa to collect data for her book, she was interested in researching the role of adolescent girls in a non-Western culture.

   _____

   _____

6. Writers often use autobiographical information to write fiction, they adapt the background of other people for their story.

   _____

   _____

Correcting run-on sentences with subordinating conjunctions

Use the subordinating conjunction in parentheses to correct the run-on sentence.

1. Ernest Hemingway wrote about the lost generation after World War I, he was living in Paris. (when)

    When Ernest Hemingway wrote about the lost generation after World

    War I, he was living in Paris.

2. Margaret Mitchell was able to write the epic novel *Gone with the Wind*, she understood the decline of the southern plantation owners. (because)

    _____

    _____

3. Somerset Maugham was a doctor, he wrote many important novels, short stories and plays. (although)

    _____

    _____

4. Some of the Harry Potter books have already been made into movies, they are so popular. (since)

    _____

    _____

5. Wallace Stevens received the Pulitzer Prize for his collected poems, he was vice president of an insurance company. (when)

    _____

    _____

Language Focus

Sentence Fragments

Look at the sentence fragment below.

When I first started college. (INCORRECT)

Avoid sentence fragments by ensuring that each dependent clause follows or precedes a main clause.

| dependent clause | | main clause |

When I first started college, I was excited about facing the challenge.

| main clause | dependent clause |

She found out **because I told her.**

Correcting sentence fragments

Rewrite each sentence fragment as a correct sentence by adding a main clause. Compare your answers with a partner.

1. Although we do not see each other very often.

   Although we do not see each other very often, my sister and I always stay
   in touch.

2. When I visited her.

   _____

3. Because she had a demanding job.

   _____

4. Since I was her favorite.

   _____

5. After she got married.

   _____

Language Focus

Verb Tense Consistency

When writing an essay, it is important to be consistent in the use of verb tense.

- When describing facts and habits, use the present tense.
  Tourists **visit** the Alamo and **enjoy** its history and beauty.

- When telling a story, use the past tense.
  On our trip to San Antonio, Texas, we **visited** the famous Alamo and **toured** the old Spanish missions.

- You may only shift from the past to the present tense if there is a logical reason for doing so. Look at the example below. The writer shifts from the past to the present tense to make a comparison between the past and the present.
  In the 19th century, the Alamo **was used** as a fortress. However, today, it **is** a popular tourist attraction.

Read the paragraph. Correct the mistakes in verb consistency. There are eight mistakes.

While I was visiting China, I experience a special kind of warmth from the people I come in contact with. I was always aware of their special quality of friendliness. I have the unique experience of being in Beijing on the night the Chinese win their bid to host the 2008 summer Olympics. On that night, I am one of a million and a half people who poured into the streets to express their joy and gratitude. I walked with them and shake hands with as many people as I could while I sang out the words: "gong xi ni ba" (congratulations). My words are always met with big smiles and enthusiastic handshakes. Those parents with kids on their shoulders, teenagers, and many others feel as if the rest of the world was welcoming them into the global community. Now I wish them the best, and I am hoping to return one day. If you take a trip to China, you will experience the same kind of hospitality.

In Part 5 you will . . .

- review the elements of an introduction and conclusion.
- review unity and coherence.
- practice correcting run-on sentences and sentence fragments.

PART 5

Putting It All Together

Exercise 1 **Examining an introduction**

Answer the questions below about this introduction.

Overcoming a Difficult Situation

Difficult life-changing experiences become the memories that stay forever in our minds. We have to learn to balance the positive and negative effects that these situations have on us. The day after I finished my first year at college, I had one of these life-changing experiences. Going on a job interview at an international bank taught me an important lesson.

---

1. Circle the hook.

2. Find the background information and write it below. _____

   _____

3. Underline the thesis statement.

4. Write the topic of the thesis statement. _____

   _____

5. Write the controlling idea of the thesis statement. _____

   _____

Exercise 2 **Reordering for coherence**

The following sentences make up body paragraph 1 of "Overcoming a Difficult Situation." Number them from 1 to 7 to show logical time order.

_____ a. Of course I was very happy to hear the good news, but I was also a little nervous.

_____ b. One wonderful day I received an unexpected phone call.

_____ c. I knew that would give a negative impression and would show that I was irresponsible.

_____ d. She wanted to set up a job interview with me.

_____ e. The following week, on the day of the interview, I was so excited that I had a hard time deciding what clothes to wear.

_____ f. It was from the manager of a very important financial institution.

_____ g. I had to really hurry once I was dressed because I did not want to arrive late.

Editing paragraphs for coherence

A. Read body paragraph 2 of "Overcoming a Difficult Situation" and edit as necessary. There are seven mistakes.

> I was in a rush to get there, I decided to take a taxi. The traffic was so horrible that the driver was in a bad mood. He closed the door, my new skirt got caught. I tried desperately to pull it out, but it ripped. I thought about asking the driver to stop, I was too embarrassed to say anything. Although I was very upset. I tried to be calm. The ride was much longer than I expected, the air conditioning was not working. I did not want anything negative to block my mind I was eager to have this job. I wanted to have a good interview and make a strong impression. Since I learned in school that first impressions are the most valuable.

B. Read body paragraph 3 of "Overcoming a Difficult Situation" and edit as necessary. There are eight mistakes.

> Finally when I arrived at the bank, I look at my skirt. The torn hem was hanging and was covered with dirt. Once inside, I go into the ladies room. I tried to wash my skirt and hold it together with a safety pin. A few minutes later, I was in the waiting room when the secretary call me. I was embarrassed and afraid that I would not get the job because of my sloppy appearance. The most interesting part was that the manager asked me what happen. When I tell her the story, she started to laugh. She can't stop. She wanted to ask me something about myself, but she keeps on laughing. Now I was sure I would not get the job. She said, "I will never forget this. I never thought that I will have such a good time today. You know, when you have to interview a lot of people in one day, it can become very boring." Despite this ordeal, she assured me that I had the right qualifications, and in the end she offered me the position.

Analyzing a conclusion

Read the conclusion to "Overcoming a Difficult Situation" and answer the questions below.

> I remember this experience because it taught me to be prepared and on time, and not to rush when I have an interview. In fact, everything that happened on that one day gave me the confidence to go forward and achieve my goals in the company. We never know when a negative experience can end up being a positive influence on our life and can stay in our minds forever.

1. Underline the sentence in the conclusion that restates the thesis from the introduction.

2. The conclusion ends with

   a. some advice.

   b. a prediction.

   c. a warning.

   d. an insight.

Identifying pronoun reference

Read the paragraph. Choose the correct pronoun to complete each sentence.

> Many people I know want attention, love, or recognition from others. Some of (they / them) get frustrated because they do not achieve
> 1.
> what they want. In my case, I wanted recognition and I got (it / him)
> 2.
> from writing. From age thirteen, I had always imagined that one day I would write short stories and become a well-known author. When I was at college, I had a good friend—Jessica Bardwell. Jessica was majoring in English composition and (her / she) encouraged me to take a creative
> 3.
> writing class. So I did, and (they / it) helped me improve my writing
> 4.
> style enormously.

Jessica would also often accompany me to poetry readings and writing workshops. Anybody could get up and present their work so I decided to present (mine / my). It was great! My classmates really
5.
helped (I / me) to feel confident about my writing. Then, close to my
6.
graduation, the college English Department invited all of (we / us) to
7.
participate in a poetry contest. My poem "Fragment of a Life" won first prize and appeared in the local newspaper. (This / These) was
8.
the beginning of my professional career as a writer. I could not have accomplished what I did without Jessica's help. I have learned from this experience that anyone can dream, but it is much easier to achieve a goal with a friend.

Exercise 6 Using transition expressions for coherence

Combine the following sentences to create coherence by using a transition word from the box.

in contrast   nevertheless   therefore   for example   moreover

1. Sometimes when essays are written too quickly the sentences do not flow naturally. You should always read your essay out loud to make sure it does.

   _____

   _____

2. The sonnets of Shakespeare always rhyme. Modern poetry usually uses free verse that does not rhyme.

   _____

   _____

3. Writing a good play requires a strong story line. You need realistic dialogue and believable characters.

   _____

   _____

4. William Shakespeare wrote comedies as well as tragedies. *The Taming of the Shrew* and *A Midsummer Night's Dream* both have happy endings.

_____

_____

5. Computers have grammar and spell check. A good writer should not depend on these tools.

_____

_____

Exercise 7 **Using parallel forms**

Rewrite the following sentences to correct the non-parallel forms.

1. A few years ago, I went to China to research a book, meet some old friends, and visiting the famous temples.

_____

_____

2. One day we toured the Ming Dynasty gardens, walked through the narrow streets, and were visiting the Great Wall.

_____

_____

3. I was eating with chopsticks, sampled spicy foods, and drank exotic teas.

_____

_____

4. The Chinese are famous for creating silk screens, paint lacquer boxes, and inventing calligraphy.

_____

_____

5. I enrolled in a Chinese culture class where I learned how to write a few characters, spoke a few words, and recognize the different tones of the language.

_____

_____

Unit 2

Process Analysis Essays

Unit Goals

Rhetorical focus:
- process analysis organization

Language focus:
- sequence connectors
- time clauses
- passives and modal passives

PART 1

Stimulating Ideas

Describing a process involves breaking it down into individual stages. In this unit you will write about a festival or holiday from your culture and explain all of its stages in logical sequential order.

| Exercise 1 | **Thinking about the topic** |

A. Discuss the pictures with a partner.

- Where do the music and dance activities in these photos take place?
- What role do you think music and dance play at this festival?
- Why are music and dance important features of many celebrations?

B. Make notes about the holidays and traditions you and your family celebrate. Then discuss in small groups.

| Exercise 2 | **Reading about the topic** |

Many countries celebrate a holiday in honor of the dead. In Japan, this holiday is known as Obon.

Obon: The Japanese Buddhist Festival of the Dead

The Japanese **Buddhist** festival of Obon is a celebration for the dead that takes place for three days in the summer. People believe that during Obon the **spirits** of their dead relatives return and the festival welcomes them home. Obon is very important to the Japanese people because ancestors are greatly respected.

Obon also celebrates the life of Mokuren Sonja, a priest famous for his supernatural powers. When he used these powers to look upon his mother, who had died, he discovered that she had fallen into the path of hungry ghosts and was greatly suffering. To save her, Sonja asked his teacher for instruction. He was told to **make offerings** to the many priests who had just completed their summer **retreat.** Because of this good deed, his mother was saved from the hungry ghosts.

During the holiday of Obon, families visit the graves of their ancestors to reunite with their ancestors' spirits. In preparation, homes are cleaned and the Buddhist altars are decorated with fruits, vegetables, sweets, and flowers. These gifts are blessed and offered to the spirits. Fires, lanterns, and incense are lit outside the houses to help guide the spirits home. When Obon is over, the fires help to send the spirits back.

On the night of the Obon matsuri, or festival, lanterns are lit and the celebration begins. Men and women dress in yukata, or light cotton summer kimonos. There are many lively activities. Crowds are entertained by folk bands and dancers, while the children are fascinated with the fireworks called hanabi-taikai. The Bon Odori, or circle dance, is enjoyed by children and adults alike.

The hot summer evenings in Japan are perfect for lively gatherings and amusement. In fact, the celebrations often continue into the early morning hours. Obon is a magical event and a favorite among many Japanese. If you are planning a trip to the Land of the Rising Sun, this is one festival not to be missed.

Adapted from "Obon: Buddist Festival of the Dead" by Lauren Clink.

Buddhist: of the Asian religion of Buddhism
make offering: give gifts

retreat: days of rest and meditation
spirits: ghosts of the dead

Exercise 3   Understanding the text

Write *T* for true or *F* for false for each statement.

_____ 1. Obon celebrates the departure of the spirits.

_____ 2. Sonja asked his teacher to help him save his dead mother.

_____ 3. Families light incense so that the spirits stay away.

_____ 4. After the Obon holiday, the fires help send the spirits back.

_____ 5. Men and women wear kimonos.

Exercise 4   Responding to the text

Write your answers for each question in full sentences. Then discuss your answers with a partner.

1. What special talent did Mokuren Sonja have? _____

_____

2. How was Sonja's mother saved? _____

_____

3. How do families prepare for Obon? _____

_____

4. Who participates in the bon-odori? _____

_____

5. What other celebrations or rituals do you know that celebrate the dead?

_____

Exercise 5   Freewriting

Write for ten to fifteen minutes on the topic below. Express yourself as well as you can. Don't worry about mistakes.

Think of a holiday that you would like to write about.

• What activities and preparations are required?

• Who participates?

• What traditions are preserved?

In Part 2 you will . . .

• learn about process analysis organization.

• brainstorm ideas and specific vocabulary to use in your writing.

• create an outline for a process analysis essay.

PART 2

Brainstorming and Outlining

✍ WRITING TASK

In this unit you will write a five-paragraph process analysis essay about the stages of a festival or holiday that you are familiar with.

Exercise 1 — Brainstorming ideas

Review your freewriting exercise. What festival or holiday will you write about? Use a graphic organizer like the one below to create a list of the preparations and activities in sequential order.

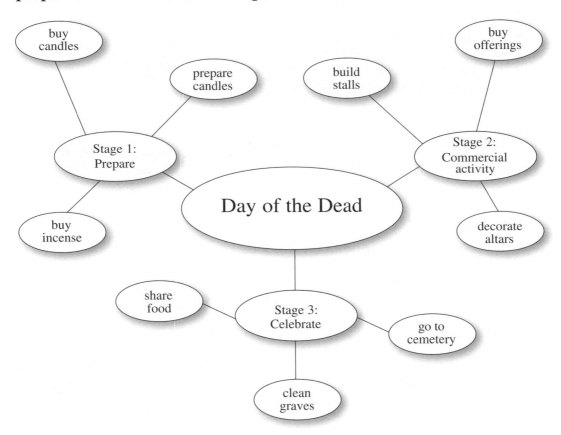

Exercise 2 — Brainstorming vocabulary

Think about the festival or holiday you will discuss in your essay. Brainstorm words for each of the categories below that are relevant to the celebration.

1. **Costumes:** _____, _____, _____

2. **Foods:** _____, _____, _____

3. **Music/Dance:** _____, _____, _____

4. **Decorations:** _____, _____, _____

Rhetorical Focus

Process Analysis Organization

A process analysis essay shows a logical progression of stages that lead to a finished product or end result. A process analysis essay might illustrate a natural process, such as photosynthesis or soil erosion. It may also describe how something is made or done, such as baking a cake, preparing for a festival, or using a computer.

Introduction
- The hook introduces the process.
- Background information helps the readers understand the process.
- The thesis statement identifies the process to be explained.

Body Paragraphs
- The topic sentence in each paragraph introduces one stage of the process.
- Each stage is organized into a logical sequence of connected steps. Body paragraphs use facts, examples, key terms, and definitions.
- All the materials needed in the process are mentioned.

Conclusion
- The conclusion gives a restatement of the process.
- It may include a final comment that is an evaluation, a recommendation, or a warning.

Exercise 3   **Reading a student essay**

Read the essay. What happens on the Mexican Day of the Dead?

Day of the Dead Celebration

Mexican culture is full of colorful traditions. One of them is the celebration of the Day of the Dead. This special holiday for remembering the dead takes place on November 2nd of every year. On that day, families believe that their dead relatives will return home to eat and drink. In my native town, Puebla, preparation begins three weeks before the holiday.

To get ready for this celebration, a number of items must be bought and prepared. People buy big and expensive candles, copal (a kind of incense), and a special native handicraft called an ensomerio in which the copal is burned. Copal is used in many religious ceremonies and on holidays like the Day of the Dead. In addition to buying candles, incense, and copal, people prepare candies. Tiny, picturesque sculptures of animals and skulls made of confectionery sugar are prepared and the names of people are engraved on the top. These candies are eaten at the end of the celebration. As a child, eating these candies was my favorite part of the Day of the Dead.

The local merchants play an important role on this day. Very early on the morning of November 2nd, they start to build stalls, to protect themselves and their products from the sunlight. Later they display their merchandise, which consists of fragrant fruit, colorful flowers, and freshly baked bread. People buy offerings for their dead relatives—these offerings include a candle, a skull made of sugar, and various types of fruit. These are all placed on an altar. People scatter yellow and red flowers on the ground to form a colorful path, which must be completed by noon. It is an indescribable pleasure to smell the exotic scent of the flowers.

At sunset, families go to the cemetery to decorate and watch over the graves of dead relatives. First the grave is cleaned and covered with flowers. Many people stay awake all night guarding the grave and keeping the dead company until the sun rises the next day. Hungry families can buy traditional food and drink at the entrance of the cemetery. They offer flowers and candles to their dead relatives.

When the celebration ends, most families share fruit and bread with friends and neighbors because they have bought too much. Some of the people who eat the fruit say that the taste is not the same because the dead have already eaten the essence, the sweetest part. Of all the religious celebrations in Mexico, this one is observed the most. Although this holiday requires a lot of planning and preparation, it is a wonderful occasion for Mexican families to reunite and remember their ancestors.

Analyzing the student essay

 A. Respond to the essay by answering the questions below in complete sentences.

 1. Why is the Day of the Dead celebrated? _____

    _____

    _____

 2. What special items are bought for this day? _____

    _____

    _____

 3. Why do the merchants build stalls? _____

    _____

    _____

 4. Why do families go to the cemetery? _____

    _____

    _____

 5. In your own words, explain why this celebration is important. _____

    _____

    _____

 B. Examine the organization of the essay by answering the questions below. Then compare your answers with a partner.

 1. Circle and label the hook.

 2. Underline the background information. What do you learn from this information? _____

    _____

    _____

 3. Circle and label the thesis statement. Rewrite it in your own words. _____

    _____

    _____

 4. What kind of process is explained in body paragraph 3? _____

    _____

    _____

 5. The last sentence in the conclusion offers
    a. an evaluation.
    b. a recommendation.
    c. a warning.

Writing an outline

Review your brainstorming ideas and freewriting exercise. Then use the chart below to write an outline for a process analysis essay on the stages of a festival or holiday that you are familiar with.

Introduction

Hook:_____

_____

_____

Background information: _____

_____

_____

Thesis statement: _____

_____

_____

process stage 1

Body Paragraph 1

Topic sentence: _____

_____

_____

Steps in sequence with explanations: _____

_____

_____

_____

_____

process stage 2

Body Paragraph 2

Topic sentence: _____

_____

_____

Steps in sequence with explanations: _____

_____

_____

_____

_____

process stage 3

Body Paragraph 3

Topic sentence: _____

_____

_____

Steps in sequence with explanations: _____

_____

_____

_____

_____

Conclusion

Restatement: _____

_____

_____

Evaluation, recommendation, or warning: _____

_____

_____

_____

_____

In Part 3 you will . . .

- learn about sequence connectors.
- learn about time clauses.
- write a first draft of your process analysis essay.

PART 3

Developing Your Ideas

Reading a student essay

Read the essay. What dish does the writer prepare?

The Thanksgiving Dinner

Three days before Thanksgiving, I went to the supermarket to do my weekly food shopping. The cashier gave me a free twenty-pound turkey because my food receipt was over fifty dollars. When I got home, I called my mother and offered to help her prepare Thanksgiving dinner by cooking the turkey. I did not know how to cook a turkey, but since I had gotten one, I decided it was a good opportunity to learn how.

Before I could begin, I had to find a recipe. I went on the Internet and looked at several cooking websites. Friends also gave me cooking advice. My goal was to make the juiciest and tastiest turkey ever. Eventually, I found a very good recipe. While I prepared the turkey, I imagined everyone at the party asking, "Who cooked such a delicious turkey?" Now I will proudly tell how to achieve such a delicacy.

A frozen turkey must be defrosted and prepared before it is roasted. First take the turkey out of the freezer and put it in the refrigerator for three days before cooking. After the turkey has been defrosted, take the plastic off and place it in a large bowl with water and seven squeezed lemons. Leave it to marinate for half an hour. Next, wash the turkey thoroughly. After this, poke the turkey with a knife and add seasoning. Try to get the freshest herbs you can find because the quality of the ingredients is highly significant. I used the following ingredients: garlic, onion, pepper, oregano, parsley, coriander, salt to taste, and three packets of Sazón Goya, a Spanish seasoning, for added flavor. All these ingredients are mixed in the blender. Finally, brush olive oil on the top part of the turkey to achieve a golden look.

No turkey is complete, however, without rich stuffing inside. There are many options to choose from. Some recipes call for rice while others use cornbread or white bread. To make a cornbread stuffing, first, follow the directions from a cornbread mix and then put the cornbread in the oven to bake. Second, while it is baking, cut some chorizo sausage, and sauté it. Then, chop some garlic and onion and sauté that until it is golden brown. As soon as the cornbread is done, take it out of the oven to cool off. Mash up the cornbread and mix all the ingredients together. Add some freshly chopped parsley and walnuts, salt, pepper, and thyme. Before you put the turkey in the oven, loosely fill the cavity with the mixture and sew the opening shut with thick thread. Finally, cook it in the oven for five hours, the recommended time for a twenty-pound turkey. There you have my personal recipe for an exquisite Thanksgiving turkey.

At my family's Thanksgiving feast, I waited patiently for their reactions as they ate dinner. But no one said anything. I hesitated but could not resist and asked what they thought of the food. They said everything was delicious, but the turkey was amazing. I told them that I had made the turkey. They were so astonished that they asked my mom if she had helped me. I explained that I had learned how to prepare and roast the turkey all by myself and explained the steps. My family was impressed by my cooking talents. As a result, I am now responsible for preparing Thanksgiving dinner next year, too!

Exercise 2   **Analyzing the student essay**

A. Respond to the essay by answering the questions in full sentences.

1. How did the writer learn how to prepare a turkey? _____

   _____

   _____

2. According to the writer, what contributes the most to making a tasty turkey? _____

   _____

   _____

3. Which two steps in the process occur at the same time? _____

_____

_____

4. What determines the cooking time for a turkey? _____

_____

_____

5. What is your favorite holiday meal? What makes it special? _____

_____

_____

B. Examine the organization of the student essay by answering the questions below. Then compare your answers with a partner.

1. Circle the hook.

2. Underline the thesis statement. Rewrite it in your own words. _____

_____

3. Write some words or phrases the writer uses to signal steps in the process.

_____

_____

_____

4. Underline all the verbs that describe the preparation and cooking process.

5. What steps are explained in body paragraph 3? _____

_____

_____

6. How is the writer's feeling of accomplishment confirmed in the conclusion?

_____

_____

_____

Language Focus

Sequence Connectors

In process analysis essays, writers need to describe the steps of a process in the order in which they occur. Sequence connectors can be used to establish a logical order. They include the words *first, second, third, next, then, before, after this,* and *finally.*

First, make sure the lights are out. **Then,** go to sleep.

Identifying sequence connectors

Read these instructions for doing laundry. Circle the sequence connectors.

How to Do the Laundry

First, collect all the dirty laundry. Second, separate the clothes into two piles: whites and colors. Third, put the clothes into the washing machine. Next, add the detergent. After this, select a wash cycle (whites, colors, delicate) and turn the machine on. Then, when the wash cycle is finished, remove the clothes and place them in the dryer. Finally, fold the clothes and put them away.

Exercise 4 **Using sequence connectors in describing a process**

A. Read these sentences from a process paragraph. Number the sentences from 1 to 6 to show a logical sequence.

How to Write a Term Paper

_____ a. Edit and revise your work.

_____ b. Write the first draft of the paper.

_____ c. Decide on a topic that you want to research.

_____ d. Organize the information in order of importance.

_____ e. Review what has been written on the topic.

_____ f. Develop a term paper outline.

B. Rewrite the sentences above into paragraph form. Use sequence connectors.

_____

_____

_____

_____

_____

Language Focus

Time Clauses

Time clauses show the order of two events. They begin with words (subordinators) that signal time order, such as are *before, after, right after* and *as soon as*. A time clause is a dependent clause and must be connected to a main clause. Time clauses can come before or after a main clause.

- When the time clause comes before the main clause, it is followed by a comma.

time clause	main clause
After the turkey has been defrosted,	take the plastic off.
Before I put the turkey in the oven,	I loosely fill the cavity.
As soon as the turkey is golden brown,	you should take it out of the oven.

- When the time clause comes after the main clause, omit the comma.

main clause	time clause
Take the plastic off	**after** the turkey has been defrosted.
I loosely fill the cavity with the mixture	**before** I put the turkey in the oven.
You should take the turkey out of the oven	**as soon as** the turkey is golden brown.

Exercise 5   Combining sentences with time clauses

Combine each pair of sentences to create a single sentence with a time clause and a main clause. Use the word in parentheses. Write the sentence two different ways.

1. Turn off your computer. Make sure to back up your work. (before)

    Before you turn off your computer, make sure to back up your work.

    Be sure to back up your work before you turn off your computer.

2. Buy a computer disk. Make sure it is compatible with your computer. (before)

3. Format it. Use the new computer disk. (before)

_____

_____

_____

_____

4. Save your essay on a disk. Print it out. (after)

_____

_____

_____

_____

5. Finish reading your e-mail. Log out. (as soon as)

_____

_____

_____

_____

6. Close all programs. Shut down the computer. (after)

_____

_____

_____

_____

Exercise 6 **Writing a first draft**

Review your outline. Then write the first draft of a five-paragraph process analysis essay about the stages of a festival or holiday.

Exercise 7 **Peer editing a first draft**

After you write your first draft, exchange it with a partner. Answer the questions on the checklist on page 47. Write comments or questions for your partner's draft. Then read your partner's comments about your first draft and revise it as necessary.

Editor's Checklist

Put a check (✓) as appropriate. Write answers in complete sentences on the lines provided.

☐ 1. Does the essay have a thesis statement that identifies the process? If so, underline the thesis statement.

☐ 2. Does the writer include background information? If so, summarize the information here. _____

_____

_____

☐ 3. Does each paragraph present a different part of the process?

☐ 4. Are the parts of the process organized in a logical sequence? List the sequence here. _____

_____

_____

☐ 5. Do the body paragraphs have any facts, definitions, or details? Tell the writer if any of these supporting details aren't sufficient. _____

_____

_____

☐ 6. Does the writer include an evaluation, recommendation, or warning in the conclusion? _____

In Part 4 you will . . .

- learn about passives.
- learn about passives without an agent.
- learn about verbs with no passive forms.
- edit your first draft for mistakes.

Editing Your Writing

Now that you have written a first draft, it is time to edit. Editing involves making changes to your writing to improve it and correct mistakes.

Language Focus

Passives

Passive sentences are often used in process analysis essays because they focus on a result or process.

- Passives are formed with *be* and a past participle. Passive verb forms are often followed by *by* + the agent (the person or thing that performs the action).
- Only sentences with transitive verbs can be changed to the passive. A transitive verb can be followed by an object.

Passive sentences change the order of the subject and object of an active sentence.

- The subject of an active sentence becomes the agent.
- The object of an active sentence becomes the subject of a passive sentence.

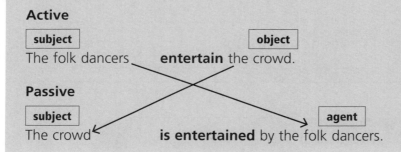

Active

| subject | | object |
The folk dancers **entertain** the crowd.

Passive

| subject | | agent |
The crowd **is entertained** by the folk dancers.

Simple Present Passive
AM/IS/ARE + PAST PARTICIPLE (+ *BY* + NOUN)
The kimono **is worn** (by women) in the summer.
The lanterns **are lit** (by families).

Modal Passive
MODAL + *BE* + PAST PARTICIPLE (+ *BY* + NOUN)
The stalls **must be built** (by the merchants).
The dead **should not be forgotten** (by the relatives).

Changing active sentences to passive

Rewrite the active sentences below as passive sentences.

1. Mexican parents buy special candies for their children.

   Special candies are bought by Mexican parents for their children.

2. The Japanese celebrate Obon in the summer.

   _____

3. The stalls protect the fragrant fruit from the sun.

   _____

4. The relatives of the dead must guard the grave.

   _____

5. The fireworks fascinate the children.

   _____

6. The merchants sell traditional food to the families.

   _____

Language Focus

Passives Without an Agent

In many passive sentences the agent can be omitted. Here are a few reasons to omit the agent.

- The agent is obvious or not important.

  Coffee is grown in Colombia.

- The agent is not known.

  A priceless artwork was stolen from the City Museum yesterday.

- The writer wants to avoid saying who is responsible for an action or event.

  The news story was leaked to the press over the weekend.

- The agent is a general noun (a person, people) or a pronoun (*someone, we, one, you,* or *they*).

  Turkey is eaten at Thanksgiving.

⚠ Be sure to use an agent when it is important to know who performed a particular action.

  Romeo and Juliet was written by Shakespeare.

Omitting agents with modal passives

Change the following sentences from active to passive. Do not include the agent.

1. People must clean gas grills properly.

   Gas grills must be cleaned properly.

2. Everyone should pick up litter and trash.

   _____

3. Parents must not allow children to play with fireworks.

   _____

4. You must cook hot dogs and hamburgers thoroughly.

   _____

5. Musicians should not play music too loudly.

   _____

6. People may display flags in front of the houses.

   _____

Including or omitting agents with passives

Change the following active sentences to passive. Omit the agent when it is not necessary.

1. People eat sushi in Japan.

   _____

2. The city government organizes many festivals.

   _____

3. Someone bakes special breads and cakes for the celebration.

   _____

4. You must defrost the turkey in the refrigerator.

   _____

5. On Saint Patrick's Day, many people in the United States wear green.

   _____

6. Merchants sell a lot of flowers and chocolates on Valentines Day.

   _____

Language Focus

Verbs With No Passive Forms

Intransitive verbs are not followed by an object and do not have a passive form. Common intransitive verbs include:

arrive	*be*	*become*
come	*disagree*	*fall*
go	*happen*	*look*
recover	*run*	*sit*
sleep	*stand*	*struggle*

Some transitive verbs also do not have passive forms. These include:

become   cost   fit   have   resemble

Exercise 4   **Recognizing verbs with no passive forms**

Change the sentences to the passive form. If the verb in the sentence does not have a passive form, write *X* next to the sentence.

_____ 1. The special costume fits Kaoru perfectly.

_____

_____ 2. The families bless the gifts offered to the spirits.

_____

_____ 3. Many cultures have special festivals in honor of the dead.

_____

_____ 4. People do not sleep well in hot weather.

_____

_____ 5. Families decorate the Buddhist altars.

_____

_____ 6. The spirits arrive during Obon.

_____

Read the paragraph. Correct the mistakes in passive structure. There are seven mistakes.

Every year, the falling autumn leaves signal the approach of Halloween. It is one of the most popular holidays in the United States, and it enjoyed by both children and adults. Many parties are held on this occasion when special costumes, masks, and wigs worn. Some of the most popular costumes that are chose are characters from children's fairy tales as well as witches, ghosts, and famous movie stars. Prizes are often given for the most unusual and creative disguises. Faces are paint with odd designs and colorful makeup. The fronts of many houses decorated with gravestones, monsters, and jack-o-lanterns. These lanterns are making from pumpkins, which are carved out to create scary faces. On the night of Halloween, children go trick-or-treating, which means going from house to house to collect candy. For kids and adults alike, Halloween is great fun. But remember, young children should to be accompanied by an adult at all times.

Exercise 6 **Editing your first draft and rewriting**

Review your essay for mistakes. Use the checklist. Then write a final draft.

Editor's Checklist

Put a check (✓) as appropriate.

☐ 1. Did you use any logical connectors?

☐ 2. Did you use any time clauses?

☐ 3. Did you use any modal passives?

☐ 4. Did you use any passives without agents?

In Part 5 you will . . .

• review the elements of process analysis writing.
• practice writing under a time limit.

Putting It All Together

In this part of the unit, you will complete five exercises to improve your accuracy, write a timed essay to improve your fluency, and explore topics for future writing.

Exercise 1 Using sequence connectors

A. Read these sentence from a process paragraph. Number the sentences from 1 to 6 to show a logical sequence.

Applying for a scholarship

_____ a. Select three or four scholarships that are appropriate for you.

_____ b. Complete the application.

_____ c. Go to the Internet and review the requirements.

_____ d. Submit the application and wait for a response.

_____ e. Check with your counselor for available scholarships.

_____ f. Request an application form.

B. Rewrite the sentences above in paragraph form. Use sequence connectors.

_____

_____

_____

_____

_____

Exercise 2 Combining sentences with time clauses

Combine each pair of sentences to create a single sentence with a time clause and a main clause. Use the words in parentheses. Write the sentence in two ways.

1. Take off your shoes. Enter a Japanese tea house. (before)

_____

_____

2. Begin the ceremony. Sit in the proper position. (after)

_____

_____

3. Pour hot water into the tea bowl. Stir the mixture. (as soon as)

_____

_____

4. Admire the design of the bowl. Taste the tea. (before)

_____

_____

5. Pass the bowl to the next person. Drink the tea. (after)

_____

_____

Exercise 3 **Changing active sentences to the passive**

Rewrite the active sentences below as passive sentences.

1. The fans idolize baseball players.

_____

_____

2. Fans can buy tickets on the Internet.

_____

_____

3. Large corporations often sponsor the games.

_____

_____

4. The umpire must wear a special vest.

_____

_____

5. Millions of viewers watch baseball on TV.

_____

_____

Exercise 4 **Using passives with and without agents**

Rewrite the active sentences below as passive sentences. Omit the agent when it is not necessary.

1. The principal must approve the changes to the schedule.

_____

_____

2. You must plug in the electrical drill.

_____

_____

3. People close banks and other businesses on national holidays.

_____

_____

4. In Idaho, people grow potatoes and other vegetables.

_____

_____

5. The *New York Times* publishes a weekend edition.

_____

_____

Exercise 5   Editing a paragraph

Read the paragraph and edit as necessary. There are seven mistakes.

In college, students have many responsibilities, and one of them is to understand the rules of the university. International students may be confused by some of these rules. For instance, on most American college campuses, alcohol consumption is prohibit because of the many alcohol-related deaths among young people. Educators believe that students should be make aware of the dangers of excessive drinking. Another issue is smoking in public spaces, which permitted in some countries around the world. In the majority of American schools, smoking is not allowing in cafeterias, dormitories, and student unions. However, in most classrooms, food and drinks may to be consumed. Before students enter a classroom or lecture hall, they are expect to turn their cell phones off. Plagiarism and cheating on exams be not tolerated; serious consequences may result.

⏱ TIMED WRITING: 60 minutes

Write a five-paragraph process analysis essay on the process of preparing for a special occasion. Before you begin to write, review the suggested time management strategy below.

Step 1 | BRAINSTORMING: 5 minutes

Write down ideas and vocabulary for your essay on a separate piece of paper. You may want to list the steps of the process in sequential order.

Step 2 | OUTLINING: 5 minutes

Write an outline for your essay.

Introduction

Hook: _____

_____

_____

_____

_____

Background information: _____

_____

_____

_____

_____

Thesis statement: _____

_____

_____

process
stage 1

Body Paragraph 1

Topic sentence: _____

_____

_____

Steps in sequence with explanations: _____

_____

_____

_____

_____

process stage 2

Body Paragraph 2

Topic sentence: _____

_____

_____

Steps in sequence with explanations: _____

_____

_____

_____

_____

process stage 3

Body Paragraph 3

Topic sentence: _____

_____

_____

Steps in sequence with explanations: _____

_____

_____

_____

_____

Conclusion

Restatement: _____

_____

_____

Evaluation, recommendation, or warning: _____

_____

_____

_____

_____

Step 3   **WRITING: 40 minutes**

Use your brainstorming notes and outline to write your first draft on a separate piece of paper.

EDITING: 10 minutes

When you have finished your first draft, check it for mistakes, using the
checklist below.

Editor's Checklist

Put a check (✓) as appropriate.

☐ 1. Does the essay have five paragraphs?

☐ 2. Is there a thesis statement that focuses the essay?

☐ 3. Does the essay explain the steps of the process in sequential order?

☐ 4. Do the body paragraphs explain the steps clearly?

☐ 5. Did you use logical connectors?

☐ 6. Did you use any time clauses?

☐ 7. Did you include any passives or modal passives?

☐ 8. Does the conclusion restate the steps in the process?

Topics for Future Writing

1. **Write a five-paragraph process analysis essay on one of the following
   topics. Use the Internet or other sources to research the topic, if
   necessary.**

   - How does the human respiratory system work?
   - What makes a volcano erupt?
   - How would you prepare for a part in a play?
   - How are laws made in your native country?
   - How does a person become a candidate to run for office in your native
     country?

2. **Write a five-paragraph process analysis essay on one of the topics
   above, but from a friend's point of view. Interview a friend,
   classmate, or relative about his or her views on the topic. Take notes
   during the interview to use for your essay.**

3. **Use the Internet or other sources to research one of the topics or a
   topic of your choice. Then write a process analysis essay based upon
   your research.**

Cause and Effect Essays

Unit Goals

Rhetorical focus:
- cause and effect organization
- relating effects to causes

Language focus:
- sentence connectors showing cause and effect
- real and unreal conditionals

PART 1

Stimulating Ideas

Many people travel great distances to find happiness. Others find happiness in the world around them. In this unit you will explore the causes of happiness.

"I've got the bowl, the bone, the big yard. I know I _should_ be happy."

Exercise 1   **Thinking about the topic**

A. Discuss the cartoon with a partner.

- What do the bowl, the bone, and the yard represent to the dogs in the cartoon?
- What is the message of the cartoon?
- How do you feel about the issues raised by the cartoon?

B. Make notes about what makes you happy. Then discuss in small groups.

Exercise 2   **Reading about the topic**

A young filmmaker from New York made a documentary about how to find happiness, "One Happy Movie," which provides some deep insights.

What Makes People Happy?
Young Filmmaker Finds the Answer

While his childhood friends stayed in Harlem in New York City, Aaron Mighty went to college. As his college **peers** spent their money on fraternities and parties, Mighty invested in the stock market. When his graduate school colleagues **sought out** teachers to ask questions, Mighty spent nearly $10,000 to get an answer.

Plagued with self-doubt and uncertainty about his future, he wondered, "What makes people happy?" He found the answer in making the feature documentary film, "One Happy Movie." The film **catalogs** a cross-country road trip by four college students visiting a variety of cities, towns, and landmarks, **posing** the question to a large number of people.

"The originality of the concept is what intrigued people," Mighty said. "When I first told people I was making a film about happiness, they **mocked** me and said, 'There's no happiness in the world,' but obviously there is. A lot of people, especially college-age people, think about it all the time. We constantly think about our direction, what our focus is, and what we want to do in life to make us happy."

The director of the project, David Acevedo, agrees and said he was **drawn to** directing the project because he wanted to see how answers would change depending on people's social, economic, and racial background.

"We got several deep responses, and many **weird** responses about what made people happy," Acevedo said. "It surprised me how people could be from so many different social or racial backgrounds, people of all ages, from small towns to big cities, rich and poor, young and old, but so many of them had such similar answers."

The young filmmaker feels satisfied that he learned the answer to the question he set off to answer years ago, regardless of how much money the film generates.

peers: people of the same age or class as others
sought out: went to look for
plagued: overwhelmed
catalogs: describes
posing: asking
mocked: made fun of
drawn to: pulled towards
weird: strange; unusual

"I know now what the answer is," Mighty said. "It is the simple things in life. It's not about what kind of car you drive, how much money you make, how big your house is. Those are things that are truly **irrelevant**, and those are things in the most part we didn't get from people. I've learned that life is just about living. It's about going out there and enjoying life and being happy."

Adapted from "What Makes People Happy" by Patricia Xavier. Reprinted with permission from Incharge Education Foundation, Inc. Jan/Feb issue of Young Money, *www.youngmoney.com.*

irrelevant: having nothing to do with the subject

Exercise 3   Understanding the text

Write *T* for true or *F* for false for each statement.

_____ 1. Aaron Mighty enjoyed fraternities and parties.

_____ 2. He was sure about his future.

_____ 3. People thought that the idea for his movie was original.

_____ 4. He was not concerned about how much money the movie would earn.

_____ 5. According to Mighty, a beautiful home, money, and a nice car will not bring happiness.

Exercise 4   Responding to the text

Write your answers for each question in full sentences. Then discuss your answers with a partner.

1. What made Mighty different from his peers?_____

_____

_____

_____

2. How did Mighty find answers to his questions?_____

_____

_____

_____

3. What were Mighty's conclusions about happiness?_____

_____

_____

_____

4. Do you agree with Mighty's conclusions? Why or why not? _____

_____

_____

_____

5. If you were to research what makes people happy, what kind of evidence would you look for? _____

_____

_____

_____

Exercise 5 **Freewriting**

Write for ten to fifteen minutes on the topic below. Express yourself as well as you can. Don't worry about mistakes.

People find happiness in different ways. How do you find happiness?
- What are some of the physical, emotional, and psychological things in life that make you happy?
- How do you express your happiness?
- How does it affect the people around you?

In Part 2 you will . . .

- learn about cause and effect organization.
- brainstorm ideas and specific vocabulary to use in your writing.
- create an outline for a cause and effect essay.

PART 2

Brainstorming and Outlining

✎ WRITING TASK

In this unit you will write a five-paragraph cause and effect essay about the physical, emotional, or psychological causes of happiness.

Exercise 1 | Brainstorming ideas

In the left column of the chart, note three different causes of happiness. In the right column, note details associated with these causes. These details may be explanations, examples, or facts.

Causes of Happiness ⟶	Details
1. _____	• _____
2. _____	• _____
3. _____	• _____

Exercise 2 | Brainstorming vocabulary

A. The vocabulary below is useful for writing about happiness. Write related words that will add details to your essay.

1. **Happiness:** fulfillment, contentment, satisfaction, peace of mind, _____, _____, _____, _____

2. **Actions:** achieve, accomplish, succeed, _____, _____, _____, _____

3. **Results:** Bring about, result in, lead to, _____, _____, _____, _____

B. Practice writing example sentences using the words above. Use a dictionary for help.

1. _Achieving job satisfaction results in feelings of contentment._

2. _____

3. _____

4. _____

5. _____

Rhetorical Focus

Cause and Effect Organization

A cause and effect essay explains why certain actions, situations, and behaviors happen. The essay can start with an effect, such as success, and find its causes, which might be education or talent. Or the essay can begin with a cause and describe its effects.

Introduction
- The hook introduces the cause(s) or effect(s).
- Background information helps the reader understand the cause(s) or effect(s). It can give historical information.
- The thesis statement shows the relationship between the cause(s) and effect(s).

Body Paragraphs
- The topic sentence in each paragraph defines a specific cause or effect to support the thesis.
- All supporting details must relate to the topic sentence. These details can include explanations, examples, or facts.
- Body paragraphs are organized in order of importance, chronologically, or according to short-term or long-term effects.
- Each paragraph must use clear logic.

Conclusion
- The conclusion restates the cause(s) and effect(s) of the essay.
- It may evaluate or reflect on the ideas presented.
- It may give advice.

Exercise 3   **Reading a student essay**

Read the essay. What are the effects of a positive outlook?

Effects of a Positive Outlook on Our Lives

Happiness is a state of being that everyone wants to achieve. A positive outlook can help you be happy and change the outcome of your life. It can enrich your relationships, improve your health, and guide you through some of life's greatest challenges.

A positive outlook helps you find happiness in professional, social, and personal relationships. Having a positive attitude will help you find a good job and keep it. Colleagues enjoy working with someone who always looks at the bright side and avoids conflict. Friends will appreciate your energy and want to spend more time with you. A happy person makes everybody else happy. It is contagious. Happiness and a positive outlook on life can also have a beneficial effect on personal relationships. As a consequence, any partnership will be a solid, strong, and happy relationship.

Having a positive outlook also makes a person healthy. In fact, medical science has proven that stress, which causes many of today's common illnesses such as high blood pressure, heart disease and cancer, can be avoided when people feel good about themselves. If you have a good sense of humor and laugh a lot, a chemical substance called serotonin will be released into your blood stream, giving you an immediate feeling of well-being and tranquillity. It has also been found that the elderly recover faster from illness when they are cheerful. Being positive and happy is synonymous with health and longevity.

Finally, people with positive outlooks are stronger and capable of confronting difficult situations. They develop clear minds, which help them cope with life's challenges better than those individuals who are not at peace with themselves. Happy people's optimism creates the strength needed to find rational solutions to the many unexpected problems that life presents. This optimism also promotes self-esteem. For example, happier students are more likely to approach professors for help when they are having some trouble in their course work. In contrast, unhappy or less happy students may internalize their frustrations and be less likely to seek out help.

In conclusion, it is a good idea to have a positive outlook and recognize what makes us happy since it will bring us more harmony. Happiness will bring us strong relationships, good health, and the ability to face any obstacle. If we promise ourselves to laugh more and think positively, we will change our lives for the better.

Exercise 4   **Analyzing the student essay**

Examine the organization of the essay by answering the questions below. Then compare your answers with a partner.

1. Circle and label the hook.

2. Underline the background information.

3. Circle the thesis statement. Rewrite it in your own words. _____

_____

_____

4. Underline the topic sentence in each body paragraph.

5. Write two details from body paragraph 3 that illustrate the effects of happiness. _____

_____

_____

6. How are the introduction and the conclusion similar? _____

_____

_____

| Exercise 5 | **Writing an outline** |

Review your brainstorming ideas and freewriting exercise. Then use the chart below to write an outline for a cause and effect essay about the physical, emotional, or psychological causes of happiness.

Introduction

Hook: _____

_____

_____

Background information: _____

_____

_____

Thesis statement showing a relation between cause and effect: _____

_____

_____

| cause 1 | **Body Paragraph 1** |

Topic sentence: _____

_____

_____

Supporting details: _____

_____

_____

cause 2 | **Body Paragraph 2**

Topic sentence: _____

_____

_____

Supporting details: _____

_____

_____

cause 3 | **Body Paragraph 3**

Topic sentence: _____

_____

_____

Supporting details: _____

_____

_____

Conclusion

Restatement: _____

_____

_____

Evaluation, reflection, or advice: _____

_____

_____

In Part 3 you will . . .

- learn more about causes and effects.
- learn about sentence connectors showing cause and effect.
- write a first draft of your cause and effect essay.

PART 3

Developing Your Ideas

Reading a student essay

Read the essay. According to the writer, what factors lead to success in college?

Factors that Lead to Success in College

The road to success in college is full of obstacles that might interfere with students reaching their goals. Despite these obstacles, students can achieve their dream of earning their degree. They need support from family and friends, strong motivation, and the ability to focus.

First, college students need the support of their families to succeed. If they are lucky, they have families that protect and nurture them. Their family members act as helping hands, friends who they can depend on emotionally. Students need this support system to help them realize their own capacity even when they doubt themselves. For example, because the work load is too great or the exams are too hard, students may get discouraged. Families can encourage them to persevere. In addition, tuition and books are very expensive; consequently, some students are forced to work. If they receive financial assistance from their families, they can dedicate all their time to their studies.

Students need to keep up the motivation they need to study. Students have many obligations to fulfill, such as completing homework assignments and research projects, studying for exams, and writing term papers. Many students work after school and arrive home late at night. Only dedicated and responsible students will push themselves to finish their work before going to bed. When the options are to go to a party with friends or stay home and work, only determined students will choose to study.

Students also need to focus on realistic academic goals. Many students are not aware of the importance of selecting the right college and major. In fact, a wrong decision may result in a waste of time and money. For example, students may have very high expectations and select a major that presents demands they cannot meet. In some cases, they find themselves on a career path they do not even enjoy. As a result, they may have to change their major or drop out of college when they realize that they cannot keep up their grades. If they are more focused on what they want, the better their chances will be to achieve their goals.

If students are enthusiastic about what they are studying, realistic about their academic goals, and receive support from their families, their college journey will be easier. They need to transform themselves into eagles. An eagle knows how to focus on what it wants and capture it even when the distance is great.

Exercise 2 **Analyzing the student essay**

Respond to the essay by answering the questions below in full sentences.

1. What are some of the obstacles that college students face? _____
   _____
   _____

2. What might prevent a student from finishing his or her college work?
   _____
   _____

3. Why can students have difficulty keeping up their motivation? _____
   _____
   _____

4. Why is it important for students to be focused? _____
   _____
   _____

5. What obstacles and successes have you experienced in your academic life?
   _____
   _____
   _____

Rhetorical Focus

Relating Effects to Causes

A cause may have many effects, but they must be logically related. Read the following paragraph about the effects of a bus strike in a city. Notice how the writer crossed out a sentence that does not relate to the cause stated in the topic sentence of the paragraph.

Bus strikes can disrupt the lives of residents in a city. When buses are on strike, many people are forced to find alternative means of transportation. Some may take taxis. However, during a strike it is often difficult to get a taxi. Other riders may create car pools to deal with the inconvenience. ~~Another effect is that public transportation can be very expensive.~~ The worst effect is when workers cannot get to their jobs and lose much needed income.

The cost of transportation is not an effect of the strike and does not belong in the paragraph.

Exercise 3 Identifying related effects

Write X next to the sentence that does not relate to the statement.

1. Being a happy person can benefit your life in many ways.

   _____ a. A happy person can make friends more easily

   _X_ b. There are many happy people all over the world.

   _____ c. Happy people can solve their problems effectively.

2. It is important to get a college education.

   _____ a. A college education provides more job opportunities.

   _____ b. A person's life-long earning capacity is increased.

   _____ c. Many colleges offer scholarships.

3. Air pollution has many negative effects.

   _____ a. An example of air pollution is car exhaust fumes.

   _____ b. Asthma rates increase in highly polluted areas.

   _____ c. Unclean air destroys the natural environment.

4. Watching too much television affects everyone.

   _____ a. It reduces the amount of time people read.

   _____ b. Research has shown that children become more aggressive.

   _____ c. Many homes have more than one TV.

5. There are many advantages to using computers.

   ____ a. Computers have become more reasonable to purchase.

   ____ b. Using computers saves time writing reports and letters.

   ____ c. The time needed to do research is greatly reduced.

Language Focus

Cause Connectors

In a cause and effect essay, connectors create coherence by indicating the relationship between ideas in sentences.

Connectors Introducing a Clause

- Use *because* or *since* to introduce a dependent clause. A dependent clause must be attached to a main clause in order to be a sentence.

- Remember, both dependent and main clauses contain a subject and a verb.

- Note that when the dependent clause comes at the beginning of the sentence, it is followed by a comma. When the dependent clause comes at the end of the sentence, no comma is used.

dependent clause	main clause
Because/Since the traffic was heavy,	we were late for class.

main clause	dependent clause
We were late for class	**because/since** the traffic was heavy.

Connectors Introducing a Noun Phrase

- Use *due to, because of,* and *as a result of* to introduce a noun phrase.

- A noun phrase is formed by a noun and its modifiers, for example, *heavy traffic*. It has no verb.

- When the noun phrase comes at the beginning of a sentence, it is followed by a comma. When the noun phrase comes at the end of a sentence, no comma is used.

Due to the **heavy traffic**, we were late for class.

We were late for class due to the **heavy traffic**.

Using connectors to introduce a clause

Combine each pair of sentences to show cause and effect. Use the connector in parentheses.

1. There have been new advances in air and space technology. We are able to travel greater distances in less time. (because)

   <u>Because there have been new advances in air and space technology, we are</u>
   <u>able to travel greater distances in less time.</u>

2. People are living longer. They are receiving better medical treatment. (since)

   _____

   _____

3. Orchestras are trying to attract a younger audience. Reduced rates at concert halls are available for many high school students. (because)

   _____

   _____

4. Research has shown that it reduces stress. More and more individuals are practicing yoga. (since)

   _____

   _____

Using connectors to introduce a phrase

Combine each pair of sentences to show cause and effect. Use the connector in parentheses. You will need to change the first sentence into a noun phrase.

1. Interest rates are low. More people are buying homes for the first time. (due to)

   <u>Due to lower interest rates, more people are buying homes for the first time.</u>

   _____

2. The pollen count is high. My allergies are very bad this season. (as a result of)

   _____

   _____

3. My work was excellent. I received the highest grade in the class. (because of)

   _____

   _____

4. The fire was destructive. The building had to be demolished. (due to)

_____

_____

Language Focus

Effect Connectors

Use _therefore_, _as a result_, or _consequently_ to introduce effect clauses. These connectors always come between two main clauses. One clause shows a cause and the other shows an effect.

- When the clauses are joined into one sentence, the connector is always preceded by a semicolon and followed by a comma.

| cause | | effect |

I studied all weekend for the test; **as a result**, I got an A.

- The connector may also begin a separate sentence. In this case, it is followed by a comma.

| cause | | effect |

I studied all weekend for the test. **Consequently**, I got an A.

Exercise 6   **Using connectors to show effect**

Combine each pair of sentences to show cause and effect. Use the connector in parentheses.

1. The picnic was cancelled. The weather was bad. (therefore)
   The weather was bad; therefore, the picnic was cancelled.

2. The fire caused major damage to the school auditorium. We will have the performance in the town hall. (consequently)

   _____

   _____

3. Many farmers moved to California. The Great Depression was devastating. (as a result)

   _____

   _____

4. Flights no longer provide meals. Airlines have cut back services. (as a result)

   _____

   _____

5. The reviews were great. The theater added more performances. (therefore)

_____

_____

Exercise 7 **Writing a first draft**

Review your outline. Then write the first draft of a five-paragraph essay about the causes of happiness.

Exercise 8 **Peer editing a first draft**

After you write your first draft, exchange it with a partner. Answer the questions on the checklist. Write comments or questions for your partner. Then read your partner's comments about your first draft and revise it as necessary.

Editor's Checklist

Put a check (✓) as appropriate. Write answers in full sentences on the lines provided.

☐ 1. Does the introduction include a general thesis about the causes and effect? Underline this statement.

☐ 2. Does each body paragraph contain a topic sentence that defines a specific cause?

☐ 3. Are the causes explained in a logical way?

☐ 4. Does the writer use connectors to show cause and effect?

☐ 5. Does the conclusion restate the causes?

☐ 6. Is there an evaluation or a reflection in the conclusion? Write it here.

_____

_____

In Part 4 you will . . .

- learn about real and unreal conditionals.
- edit your first draft.

PART 4
Editing Your Writing

Now that you have written a first draft, it is time to edit. Editing involves making changes to your writing to improve it and correct mistakes.

Language Focus

Conditional Sentences

Conditional sentences express cause and effect. A conditional sentence has a dependent if clause and a main clause. There are two types of conditional sentences: real and unreal.

Real Conditionals

Real conditionals express situations that may or may not happen. The *if* clause describes a possible condition or event. The main clause shows a possible result.

- Use the simple present in the *if* clause of a real conditional. In the main clause, use the simple present, *will*, or *can, should, may* depending on how certain you are about the result. You may also use the imperative in the main clause to give an order.

- When the *if* clause is first, use a comma. You may also use the word *then* before the main clause. When the main clause is first, do not use a comma.

  If I get the new job, (then) I will make more money.
  I will make more money if I get the new job.

- In conditional sentences, either clause or both clauses can be negative.

  If I am not on time, I take the bus.
  If I am not on time, I will not walk to work.

Real Conditionals						
IF CLAUSE		MAIN CLAUSE		IF CLAUSE		MAIN CLAUSE
IF + SIMPLE PRESENT	*(THEN)*	**SIMPLE PRESENT**		**IF + SIMPLE PRESENT**	*(THEN)*	**WILL FUTURE**
If I **leave** at 8,	(then)	I **catch** the bus.		If we **are** late,	(then)	we **will call** you.
IF + SIMPLE PRESENT	*(THEN)*	**IMPERATIVE**		**IF + SIMPLE PRESENT**	*(THEN)*	**MODAL**
If you **do not feel** well,	(then)	**stay** in bed.		If you **do not hurry,**	(then)	you **may be** late.

| Exercise 1 | **Using real conditionals**

Change each statement below into a real conditional sentence. Use *will*, *can*, *should*, or *may* in the main clause.

1. Take a computer course and have better job opportunities.

   If you take a computer course, you will have better job opportunities.

2. Study hard and pass the test.

   _____

3. Get a roommate and share the rent.

   _____

4. Go to bed early and wake up refreshed.

   _____

5. Read more and increase your vocabulary.

   _____

Language Focus

Unreal Conditionals

Unreal conditional sentences express imaginary situations. The *if* clause describes a condition or event that is not true at the time of writing. The main clause shows the imaginary result of this condition.

- Use the simple past in the *if* clause of an unreal conditional. In the main clause, use *would, could,* or *might.*

- When the *if* clause is first, use a comma. When the main clause is first, do not use a comma.

If she studied harder, she would get better grades.

She would get better grades if she studied harder.

Unreal Conditionals		
┌─IF CLAUSE─┐		┌─MAIN CLAUSE─┐
IF + SIMPLE PAST	**(THEN)**	**WOULD + VERB**
If I **had** a car,	(then)	I **would ride** to work.
IF + SIMPLE PAST	**(THEN)**	**COULD + VERB**
If we **had** more money,	(then)	we **could buy** a car.
IF + SIMPLE PAST	**(THEN)**	**MIGHT + VERB**
If I **had** more time off	(then)	I **might drive** to Florida.

Exercise 2 Using unreal conditionals

Write meaningful unreal conditional sentences. Use the words given.

1. snow in Hawaii / go skiing

   If it snowed in Hawaii, people could go skiing.

2. travel by bus / own a car

   _____

3. watch a lot of TV / read books

   _____

4. know how to cook / make dinner for the whole family

   _____

5. have a lot of rain in the spring / not go camping

   _____

Exercise 3 Using real and unreal conditionals

Complete these sentences with your own ideas. Remember to use commas where needed. Compare your answers with a partner.

1. If the economy improves, _more people will have jobs_____.
2. I would buy a beach house _____.
3. If people receive better health care, _____.
4. I would learn a foreign language _____.
5. If home owners used solar energy, _____.

Editing a paragraph

Read the paragraph. Correct the mistakes in real and unreal conditionals. There are seven mistakes.

> If you liked music, think about taking a music appreciation course. If you would have any talent in that direction, you may want to join a choir. I joined a choir two years ago and I enjoy it very much. I know that if I didn't have my rehearsals, I will be very unhappy. I look forward to working with a conductor, learning challenging pieces and singing with a group. If I missed a rehearsal, I feel a little depressed. Even if we work on a difficult piece, I would find the challenge exhilarating. If music is not the hobby for you, you should found one that can bring you happiness. If you do, you would not be sorry.

Exercise 5   **Editing your first draft and rewriting**

Review your essay for mistakes. Use the checklist. Then write a final draft.

Editor's Checklist

Put a check (✓) as appropriate.

- ☐ 1. Did you use any real conditionals?
- ☐ 2. Did you remember to use *will* in the main clause for real conditional sentences?
- ☐ 3. Did you use any unreal conditionals?
- ☐ 4. Did you remember to use the past tense in the *if* clause for unreal conditional sentences?
- ☐ 5. Did you use any modals in the main clause for unreal conditional sentences?

In Part 5 you will . . .

- review the elements of cause and effect writing.
- practice writing under a time limit.

In this part of the unit, you will complete six exercises to improve your accuracy, write a timed essay to improve your fluency, and explore topics for further writing.

Exercise 1 **Identifying related causes and effects**

Write _X_ next to the sentence that does not relate to the statement.

1. Strong economic growth in a country achieves many desired goals.
   _____ a. More people buy houses.
   _____ b. Strong economic growth followed World War I.
   _____ c. There is less unemployment.

2. Weather can influence your life.
   _____ a. Weather conditions in the world are changing.
   _____ b. Cool climates promote hard work.
   _____ c. In rainy climates people are often depressed.

3. Automobiles have changed the way people live.
   _____ a. They offer increased mobility.
   _____ b. Many cars have air-conditioning.
   _____ c. They save commuting time.

4. Good parenting has many positive effects.
   _____ a. Children treat others with respect.
   _____ b. It promotes academic success.
   _____ c. Good parenting takes a lot of time.

5. Pet ownership offers many rewards.
   _____ a. Dogs, cats, and hamsters are popular household pets.
   _____ b. Having a pet prevents many common illnesses.
   _____ c. Children learn how to be responsible.

6. Listening to loud music has its consequences.
   _____ a. Stress levels can increase significantly.
   _____ b. The ability to concentrate is reduced.
   _____ c. Young people all over the world listen to loud music.

Using connectors to show cause

Combine each pair of sentences with the connector in parentheses to show cause. You may need to change one of the sentences into a noun phrase.

1. The construction industry is thriving. There is a high demand for new housing. (since)

   _____

   _____

2. Many young adults want to go to college. The competition for jobs has become fierce. (because of)

   _____

   _____

3. People are living longer. Second careers are more common. (because)

   _____

   _____

4. Newspapers and magazines are losing subscribers. Readers obtain more up-to-date information from the Internet. (since)

   _____

   _____

5. There is a great need for nurses. Many students are entering the profession. (due to)

   _____

   _____

6. The Suez Canal was built. Ships are able to travel faster from the west to the east. (as a result of)

   _____

   _____

Using connectors to show effect

Combine each pair of sentences with the connector in parentheses.

1. People are cooking less. Microwaves are time-saving. (therefore)

   _____

   _____

2. More police patrol the streets. Crime rates are high. (consequently)

   _____

   _____

3. Globalization is increasing. English has become a more popular language. (as a result).

_____

_____

4. Consumers have more choices. Shopping malls are huge. (consequently)

_____

_____

5. Cell phones are convenient and economical. Many people have cancelled their home service. (as a result)

_____

_____

6. The exam was challenging. Many students failed. (therefore)

_____

_____

Exercise 4   **Using real conditionals**

Change the following statements into real conditional sentences.

1. Work hard and succeed in your career.

_____

_____

2. Work at a job you like and accomplish more in less time.

_____

_____

3. Travel around the world and learn about new cultures.

_____

_____

4. Have a DVD drive and be able to watch movies on your computer.

_____

_____

5. Plant perennials and have flowers again next year.

_____

_____

6. Purchase tickets online and save money.

_____

_____

Using unreal conditionals

Write meaningful unreal conditional sentences. Use the words given.

1. play an instrument / you cannot join an orchestra

   _____

   _____

2. have a long semester / have less vacation time

   _____

   _____

3. have a microwave / cook everything on the stove

   _____

   _____

4. own a laptop / work efficiently

   _____

   _____

5. have any credit cards / pay with cash

   _____

   _____

Editing a paragraph

Read the paragraph and edit as necessary. There are six mistakes.

> Today, people work long hours and have too many responsibilities; as a result, they have very little leisure time. If people spent more time with family and friends, they will be happier. Often parents do not have enough time to spend with their children. Therefore, young children do not receive the parental attention they need. If parents have more home time, they could play games with their children, and participate in more school activities. If parents spend more time with their children, children would do better in school. Furthermore, if workers had more leisure time, they can go on more family vacations. Teenagers had more time to communicate with their parents if they did not have so many responsibilities. If leisure time increase, the family unit would be stronger and society as a whole would benefit.

⏱ TIMED WRITING: 60 minutes

Write a five-paragraph essay on the causes of stress in our society today. Before you begin to write, review the suggested time management strategy below.

Step 1 | **BRAINSTORMING: 5 minutes**

Write down ideas and vocabulary for your brainstorm on a separate piece of paper.

Step 2 | **OUTLINING: 5 minutes**

Write an outline for your essay.

Introduction

Hook: _____

_____

_____

Background information: _____

_____

_____

Thesis statement showing a relation between cause and effect: _____

_____

_____

cause 1 | ### Body Paragraph 1

Topic sentence: _____

_____

_____

Supporting details: _____

_____

_____

cause 2 | ### Body Paragraph 2

Topic sentence: _____

_____

_____

Supporting details: _____

_____

_____

cause 3 | **Body Paragraph 3**

Topic sentence: _____

_____

_____

Supporting details: _____

_____

_____

Conclusion

Restatement: _____

_____

_____

Evaluation, reflection, or advice: _____

_____

_____

Step 3 | **WRITING: 40 minutes**

Use your brainstorming notes and outline to write your first draft on a separate piece of paper.

Step 4 | **EDITING: 10 minutes**

When you have finished your first draft, check it for mistakes, using the checklist.

Editor's Checklist

Put a check (✓) as appropriate.

☐ 1. Does the essay have five paragraphs?

☐ 2. Does the introduction include a general thesis about the causes and effect?

☐ 3. Does each body paragraph contain a topic sentence that defines a specific cause?

☐ 4. Does the essay include connectors to show cause and effect?

☐ 5. Are all the conditional verbs in the correct form?

☐ 6. Does the conclusion restate the causes?

1. **Write a five-paragraph cause and effect essay on one of the following topics.**

   - Choose a famous person to write about such as Gandhi, Eleanor Roosevelt, Mother Teresa, or Nelson Mandela. What effects did this person have on his/her country and on the world? What are the factors in this person's life that led him or her to become such a powerful figure?
   - Choose a historical event or period, such as the Great Depression, the Meji Period, the French Revolution, or the Cultural Revolution. Write about either their causes or the effects.
   - Choose a natural phenomenon, like the Dust Bowl, an earthquake, or the plague, and discuss what the causes and effects were on society.

2. **Write a five-paragraph cause and effect essay on one of the topics above, but from a friend's point of view. Interview a friend, classmate, or relative about his or her views on the topic. Take notes during the interview to use for your essay.**

3. **Use the Internet or other sources to research one of the topics or a topic of your choice. Then write a cause and effect essay based on your research.**

Argumentative Essays

Unit Goals

Rhetorical focus:
- argumentative organization
- counter-arguments
- refutations

Language focus:
- concessions
- connectors showing addition and contrast
- adverbial clauses
- noun clauses

Every day we are faced with ethical questions about what we think
is right or wrong. In this unit you will express your opinion about
whether or not it should be legal to download or share copyrighted
property from the Internet.

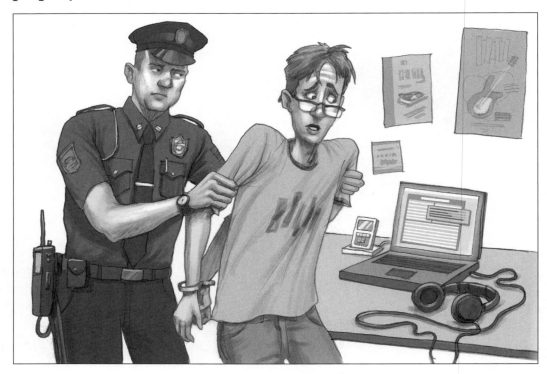

Exercise 1   Thinking about the topic

A. Discuss the picture with a partner.

- Who are the two characters in this picture?
- What do you think is happening?
- Do you think the young man is guilty of a crime?

**B. Make notes about the kinds of copyrighted property people
download off the Internet and whether or not you think
downloading should be legal. Then discuss in small groups.**

Exercise 2   Reading about the topic

Many countries today are concerned about the ethics of downloading
and sharing movies off the Internet. The case of Yoshihiro Inoue
may make some people think twice before downloading copyrighted
material off the Internet.

Japanese Man Found Guilty of Online Movie Theft

For the first time a Japanese court has found a man guilty of **piracy** and sentenced him to a year in jail. Yoshihiro Inoue, 42, downloaded movies off the Internet. He made copies of the movie *A Beautiful Mind,* and then shared them with others. This is considered a crime in the U.S., Japan, and most other countries in the world. Inoue's case sets a **precedent** for anyone who distributes films illegally. His crime was stealing intellectual property. This kind of property, which is someone's creative invention, is protected by **copyright** law.

Today over eighty nations have copyright laws. These laws protect filmmakers, writers, photographers, and other innovative professionals. People who download and copy these works often do not understand or care about the financial loss to many of these artists. To protect artistic works within the U.S., the Copyright Act of 1976 was created. Most recently the Family Entertainment and Copyright Act of 2005 was signed into law. In addition, there are **treaties** and conventions to protect intellectual property between nations. One of these is the Universal Copyright Convention. Without these laws, piracy would go **unchecked**. Some of the many types of piracy include making DVDs, duplicating VHS tapes, using hand-held video cameras in movie theaters, and even receiving satellite signals without authorization.

Yoshiro Inoue is not the first person to steal intellectual property, but he is the first to be charged with a crime for doing it. The movie industry in Hollywood and Asia are particularly interested in this case because they have a lot to lose. For a number of years the recording industry has **pursued** anyone downloading music from the Internet. Now the movie industry is following their example because piracy costs them almost $3 billion each year.

piracy: copying and selling someone else's property illegally
precedent: an example for the future
copyright: legal ownership of a creative work
treaties: legal agreements between countries
unchecked: letting something get worse because it goes without notice
pursued: gone after

A major film costs about $80 million—$55 million to make and $27 million to advertise and market. Although many people believe that the film industry makes enormous profits, almost half of all films do not earn enough money to pay back their investors. If people continue to download movies off the Internet instead of paying to see them, the movie industry will have trouble surviving.

"Japanese Man Jailed for Online Movie Piracy in Hollywood Crackdown." Agence France Press, December 2004.

| Exercise 3 | **Understanding the text** |

Write *T* for true or *F* for false for each statement.

_____ 1. Inoue was an employee of a Hollywood studio.

_____ 2. Copying movies is a crime in most countries.

_____ 3. Fewer than eighty nations protect artistic works.

_____ 4. The recording industry started prosecuting pirates before the movie industry did.

_____ 5. These thefts could cost the movie industry almost $27 million a year.

_____ 6. People who invest in movies always make money.

| Exercise 4 | **Responding to the text** |

Write your answers for each question in full sentences. Then discuss your answers with a partner.

1. Why was this arrest so important? _____

_____

_____

_____

2. What is the function of the Universal Copyright Convention? _____

_____

_____

_____

3. Why is the movie industry so afraid of the downloading and sharing of films? _____

_____

_____

_____

4. Do you think Yoshiro Inoue should have gone to jail for Internet piracy? Why? _____

_____

_____

_____

5. What kind of punishment do you think should be used against people who commit Internet piracy? _____

_____

_____

_____

| Exercise 5 | **Freewriting**

Write for ten to fifteen minutes on the topic below. Express yourself as well as you can. Don't worry about mistakes.

According to the movie industry, people who download and distribute copyrighted materials should go to jail. What do you think of the movie industry's decision?

- Do you think the law should intervene in these cases?
- How are new technologies making it so difficult to enforce the law or easy for people to break the law?
- Do you think enforcement of the laws will be difficult?

In Part 2 you will . . .

- learn about argumentative organization.
- brainstorm ideas and specific vocabulary to use in your writing.
- create an outline for your argumentative essay.

PART 2

Brainstorming and Outlining

✍ WRITING TASK

In this unit you will write a five-paragraph argumentative essay about whether or not you think it should be legal to download or share copyrighted material from the Internet.

Exercise 1 **Brainstorming ideas**

A. Review your freewriting exercise. Then, in a small group, discuss the following questions. Record your answers in a notebook.

1. What does private property mean to you?
2. What are some of the basic types of information found on the Internet?
3. What information on the Internet should be free to download?
4. What are some arguments against downloading artistic property from the Internet?
5. What are some arguments for downloading artistic property from the Internet?

B. Have you changed your position as a result of the discussion? Review the information you collected in your notebook. Underline any useful or interesting ideas. Cross out any ideas you do not want to use in your essay.

Exercise 2 **Brainstorming vocabulary**

A. Use the chart below to categorize the words and phrases.

own a copyright   commit a crime
possession   download
~~legal~~   share files
break the rules   program

law	property	computers
legal		

B. Think back to the vocabulary your group used in Exercise 1 above. Can you add any words to the chart above?

Rhetorical Focus

Argumentative Organization

An argumentative essay is sometimes called a persuasive essay. This kind of essay expresses an opinion about a controversial issue. As the writer, you must take a position and persuade the reader to agree with your opinion by using strong, logical reasons to support your argument.

Introduction
- The hook introduces the issue.
- Background information gives a broader picture of the issue and why it is important. It can give details about the history of the people involved, what they want, and how it affects them.
- The thesis statement clearly states the writer's point of view about the issue.

Body Paragraphs
- The topic sentence in each body paragraph presents one distinct reason for the writer's point of view stated in the thesis.
- All supporting details in each paragraph must support the topic sentence. These details can be facts, examples, statistics, definitions, causes and effects, quotations, anecdotes, or questions.
- The writer often presents an opposing opinion (a counter-argument); however, the writer may then express some agreement with the opposing view (a concession), but will show evidence that the argument is stronger (a refutation). The counter-argument is often in body paragraph one or three.

Conclusion
- The conclusion restates the argument that appeared in the thesis.
- It can end with a prediction, a warning, or other type of comment that reinforces the writer's viewpoint.
- It may state the general issue in a broader context.

Exercise 3 **Reading a student essay**

Read the essay below. What rules does the title refer to?

Breaking the Rules

College and high school students often look for shortcuts to make their work easier. To achieve a good grade, students are sometimes tempted to cheat. One of the most frequent ways of cheating is to buy essays off the Internet. This may result in a good grade. However, plagiarism is irresponsible from a social and an academic standpoint.

First, plagiarism is socially unacceptable. Students are expected by teachers and their classmates to do their own work. If a student plagiarizes, he or she violates that trust. This may damage the relationship between the student and the teacher, as well as the relationship with classmates. I remember once when a student was discovered to have plagiarized his essay. We were mad that our classmate had lied to us. It was an embarrassment for everyone—the institution, the instructor and the student—to discover that he had been cheating all along.

Plagiarism is also wrong because it is against academic policy. Even though buying essays and presenting them as your own may save time initially, this practice is against university rules. In fact, universities have ways to prove if students have plagiarized. Instructors can use software that compares a student essay and material on the Internet. This way, instructors can detect if a particular essay was copied. The consequences are very serious. I remember when one of my classmates started buying essays to prove that he was an excellent student. After the final exam, our instructor found his essay on a website and the student was expelled.

It is true that many students at community colleges have busy schedules and may have trouble completing their assignments on time. Some students may argue that because of their situation, they sometimes have no choice but to buy essays off the Internet. However, buying essays off the Internet should never be the solution. Instead, students might try to negotiate the deadline with their instructor. Furthermore, while writing may be a struggle for some students who feel that their writing is not good enough to receive an A, it is crucial that they do their own work. They may go to a writing center for help. Otherwise, if they plagiarize, they will not develop their own writing and critical thinking skills. As a result, they may not be prepared to pass their final exams. In the end, plagiarizing is harmful to a student's own academic success.

I believe that university authorities should discourage plagiarism by making students more aware of the problems it causes. Plagiarism damages classroom relationships. It also violates school policies and prevents students from realizing their own potential. If we do not stop plagiarism, many students will lose out on their education.

Exercise 4 **Analyzing the student essay**

A. **Respond to the student essay above by answering the questions below in complete sentences.**

1. Why do some students plagiarize? _____

_____

_____

2. How would you describe the writer's personal feelings about people who plagiarize? What makes you say that? _____

_____

_____

3. What are the negative effects of plagiarizing on students' learning skills? _____

_____

_____

4. Do you agree or disagree with the writer? Write your opinion and reasons below _____

_____

_____

5. Did the writer influence your position? If so, which point influenced you the most? _____

_____

_____

B. **Examine the organization of the essay by answering the questions below. Then compare your answers with a partner.**

1. Circle and label the hook.

2. Underline the thesis. Rewrite it in your own words. _____

_____

_____

3. What kind of supporting details are used in body paragraph 2?
   a. facts
   b. causes and effects
   c. statistics
   d. an anecdote

4. In body paragraph 3, the writer presents an opposing opinion. Rewrite it in your own words. _____

   _____

   _____

5. How many reasons has the writer restated in the conclusion? Underline the reasons.

Exercise 5   **Writing an outline**

Review your brainstorming ideas and freewriting exercise. Then use the chart to write an outline for an argumentative essay about whether or not you think it should be legal to download or share copyrighted material from the Internet.

Introduction

Hook: _____

_____

_____

Background information: _____

_____

_____

Thesis statement: _____

_____

_____

reason 1   **Body Paragraph 1**

Topic sentence: _____

_____

_____

Supporting details: _____

_____

_____

reason 2 | **Body Paragraph 2**

Topic sentence: _____

_____

_____

Supporting details: _____

_____

_____

reason 3 | **Body Paragraph 3**

Topic sentence: _____

_____

_____

Supporting details: _____

_____

_____

Conclusion

Restatement: _____

_____

_____

Prediction, warning, or issue in broader context: _____

_____

_____

In Part 3 you will . . .

- learn about counter-arguments, refutations, and concessions.
- learn about connectors showing addition and contrast.
- write a first draft of your argumentative essay.

PART 3

Developing Your Ideas

Reading a student essay

Read the essay. Why does the author think people should have free cable service?

Getting Free Cable

Everyone likes to watch TV. In fact, today almost all homes are connected to some form of cable. However, cable service is overpriced. There is a cheaper alternative called digital satellite TV. Unfortunately it is not available in every building. Because viewers have limited options and because cable companies are overcharging for their services, I believe that viewers have a right to use free unauthorized cable service.

In my opinion, cable companies charge a ridiculous amount of money for their services. For example, the family plan package starts at about $50 per month, has a separate installation fee, and does not even include the movie channels. This discounted price is only good if you are a new customer. Once this initial period is over, the price for the same service increases to more than $60 per month. To add different movie channels you have to buy a package for $15 extra. These packages consist of nine to eleven channels. However, only two of the nine are usually worth watching. Most of the movies shown are old and constantly repeated. Consequently, customers are encouraged to get other packages to obtain the channels they want. The service is simply not worth paying for.

Satellite service is not a good option for viewers. Although it is cheaper, the quality is inferior. For example, images on TV may be disturbed by the weather. In addition, many buildings do not allow tenants to use satellite dishes because strong wind, snow, or rainstorms can knock down the dish and cause an accident. An individual cannot order satellite unless a majority of the tenants agree. Therefore, I see no other option than to use the cable signal illegally.

Cable companies complain that they are losing money and that obtaining free cable is unlawful. I understand their point of view. However, a number of people, including myself, are willing to take desperate measures to get free service. We feel that these companies have a monopoly. Because there is only one cable company in each area, the company has no competition and can charge what it wants. This is not fair.

In conclusion, I think that people should be allowed to use unauthorized cable service unless we have reasonable options. The legal options we have now are not good enough, since cable is overpriced and satellite TV is inferior. Unless cable companies lower their fees, they will lose more and more paying customers and will eventually put themselves out of business.

Exercise 2   **Analyzing the student essay**

Respond to the student essay by answering the questions below in full sentences.

1. What is the first reason the writer gives for using unauthorized cable service? Explain in your own words. _____

   _____

2. What facts does the writer present in support of his argument? Explain how they strengthen the argument. _____

   _____

3. What are some of the problems with satellite service? _____

   _____

4. What are the arguments cable companies have against using unauthorized cable service? _____

   _____

5. Do you agree with the writer's opinion that people should be allowed to use unauthorized cable service? _____

   _____

Rhetorical Focus

Counter-Argument, Concession, and Refutation

The goal of an argumentative essay is to convince the reader of the writer's point of view. To make an argumentative essay strong, the writer includes a counter-argument, a refutation, and concession.

- The counter-argument is the writer's opinion about the opposing point of view. It gives reasons why the writer's point of view makes sense. By including the counter-argument, the writer shows an understanding of the opposing point of view.

- In a concession the writer agrees that the opposing point of view is valid, but emphasizes how his or her argument is still stronger.

- The refutation is the writer's response to the counter-argument. In the refutation, the writer shows why the counter-argument is weak and his or her position is strong. The refutation may also address doubts the reader may have about the writer's position.

Look at the examples below:

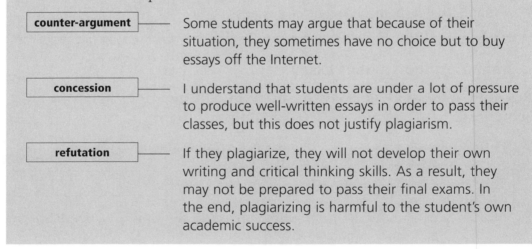

counter-argument — Some students may argue that because of their situation, they sometimes have no choice but to buy essays off the Internet.

concession — I understand that students are under a lot of pressure to produce well-written essays in order to pass their classes, but this does not justify plagiarism.

refutation — If they plagiarize, they will not develop their own writing and critical thinking skills. As a result, they may not be prepared to pass their final exams. In the end, plagiarizing is harmful to the student's own academic success.

<u>Exercise 3</u> **Identifying refutations and concessions**

Write *R* for each argument showing a refutation and *C* for each item showing concession.

_____ 1. Some students photocopy chapters of books required for their courses and believe they are justified because books are so expensive. Not only is this illegal, but it also shows a lack of intellectual curiosity.

_____ 2. Manufacturers often justify copying famous designer articles such as handbags and jewelry because they can sell them far below the cost of the original. If consumers can't tell the difference, why should this be illegal?

_____ 3. Cabaret performers often use copyrighted songs for their shows and complain about having to pay royalties and fees to the copyright owner. Since these shows are performed in front of small audiences, and these performers do not make much money, it seems unfair for them to pay.

_____ 4. Some producers have taken other peoples' story lines for movies and adapted them for their own films. They argue that their version is significantly different from the idea first presented to them. However, this practice is unethical and dishonest; therefore, the original creator should be compensated.

_____ 5. Robert's brother Jerry helped him write a college term paper a few years ago. Now Jerry feels that he has the right to submit the same term paper for his college course. Since Jerry helped write Robert's report, he is part author and should be able to receive credit for it.

_____ 6. A pastry chef working in a cupcake bakery learned new recipes from the café's head baker. When he opened his own cupcake shop across the street, he insisted on using the same recipes from his previous job. He was wrong to take recipes created by another baker and use them in his new business.

Language Focus

Connectors to Show Addition and Contrast

In order to construct a strong argument, it may be necessary to provide additional information, or to contrast different pieces of information. Addition and contrast connectors link ideas between two main clauses and clarify the relationships between ideas.

Connectors That Show Addition

- Use the connectors *furthermore, in addition,* or *moreover* to indicate additional information.

- When the clauses are joined in one sentence, the connector is always preceded by a semicolon and followed by a comma.

  The U.S. created the Copyright Act of 1976 to protect artistic works; **in addition,** there are treaties to protect intellectual properties between nations.

- An addition connector may also begin a separate sentence. In this case it is followed by a comma.

  The U.S. created the Copyright Act of 1976 to protect artistic works. **Moreover,** there are treaties to protect intellectual properties between nations.

Connectors That Show Contrast

- Use the connectors *nevertheless* or *however* to show contrast.

- When the clauses are joined in one sentence, the connector is always preceded by a semicolon and followed by a comma.

  Students who struggle with their writing might be tempted to plagiarize**;** **however,** it is crucial that they do their own work.

- A contrast connector may also begin a separate sentence. In this case it is followed by a comma.

  Students who struggle with writing their papers might be tempted to plagiarize. **However,** it is crucial that they do their own work.

Exercise 4 | **Using connectors to indicate additional information or contrast**

Combine the two sentences with a connector to indicate additional information or contrast. Check your punctuation carefully.

1. Patents are important because they protect the inventions of individuals. They are generally good for only 20 years.

   Patents are important because they protect the inventions of individuals;
   however, they are generally good for only 20 years.

2. Once an invention is patented, only the owner can make, sell, or distribute the product. Anyone else who wants to profit from this item must get permission from the owner.

   _____

   _____

3. Novels, plays, newspapers, and other original printed materials are protected by copyright law. Visual images such as drawings, photographs, and cartoons are still illegally copied off the Internet.

   _____

   _____

4. There continues to be illegal videotaping of movies in public movie theaters. The U.S. Congress found it necessary to pass the Family Copyright Act of 2005.

_____

_____

Exercise 5   Writing a first draft

Review your outline. Then write the first draft of a five-paragraph argumentative essay about downloading and sharing music off the Internet.

Exercise 6   Peer editing a first draft

After you write your first draft, exchange it with a partner. Answer the questions on the checklist. Write comments or questions for your partner. Then read your partner's comments about your first draft and revise it as necessary.

Editor's Checklist

Put a check (✓) as appropriate.

- ☐ 1. Does the essay have five paragraphs?
- ☐ 2. Does the essay have a thesis statement that identifies the writer's point of view?
- ☐ 3. Do the body paragraphs include topic sentences that support the writer's position?
- ☐ 4. Does the third body paragraph contain a counter-argument with either a refutation or a concession?
- ☐ 5. Do the details in the body paragraphs support reasons stated in the topic sentences?
- ☐ 6. Does the conclusion restate the thesis in different words, make a prediction, or state the issue in a broader context?

In Part 4 you will . . .

- • learn about adverbial clauses.
- • learn about noun clauses.
- • edit your first draft for mistakes.

Editing Your Writing

Now that you have written a first draft, it is time to edit. Editing involves making changes to your writing to improve it and correct mistakes.

Language Focus

Adverbial Clauses

An adverbial clause is a dependent clause. It is always attached to a main clause. Just as adverbs modify verbs, adverbial clauses modify the verb of the main clause to show time, place, reason, or purpose.

- All adverbial clauses must contain a subordinator (a word linking the adverbial clause to the main clause), a subject, and a verb.

- The adverbial clause can come before or after the main clause, but the punctuation is different. Use a comma after an adverbial clause when it begins a sentence.
  While summers are hot in Miami, they are cool in Seattle.
  Summers are cool in Seattle **while they are hot in Miami.**

Adverbial Clauses to Show Contrast and Concession

In order to make your argumentative essay as persuasive as possible, you will need to contrast two points of view effectively. You will also need to make concessions to opposing points of view. Use adverbial clauses to show contrast or concession.

- Begin an adverbial clause with *while* or *whereas* to show contrast. The information in the adverbial clause comes in opposition to the information in the main clause.
  While some people like to invest their savings, most people prefer to keep their money in saving accounts.
  Some students rely on buying essays off the Internet **whereas** others believe it should never be an option.

- Begin an adverbial clause with *although* or *even though* to show concession. The information in the adverbial clause presents a concession to the information in the main clause.
  Although satellite service is cheaper than cable, the quality is inferior.
  Some students buy essays and present them as their own **even though** it is against university rules.

Using adverbial clauses to show contrast or concession

Add a main clause to the following adverbial clauses to create sentences that show contrast or concession. Check your punctuation carefully.

1. while some people prefer to buy name-brand drugs

   While some people prefer to buy name-brand drugs, others choose generic
   brands because they are cheaper.

2. whereas some people like to go to a movie theater

   _____

   _____

3. even though baseball is the most popular sport in America

   _____

   _____

4. while shopping online is very convenient

   _____

   _____

5. although air travel is expensive

   _____

   _____

Language Focus

Noun Clauses

Noun clauses are dependent clauses that function as nouns in a sentence and are connected to a verb phrase. They have a subject and a verb but do not express a complete idea by themselves.

I believe **what he told me**.   I demand **that he apologize**.

Noun Clauses with *What*

We can use noun clauses that begin with *what* to express thoughts or opinions.

• A noun clause with *what* can be the subject or object of a sentence

subject	object

What he told me is not true.   I do not believe **what he told me**.

Noun Clauses with *That*

Noun clauses with *that* can be used to express an opinion or give a recommendation.

- Noun clauses with *that* can follow a verb phrase or an adjective.

- *That* can generally be omitted.
  I believe **(that) the strike will go ahead**.

- When the noun clause follows the adjectives *important, crucial, mandatory, vital,* and *essential,* or the verbs *suggest, advise, demand, insist, purpose, argue,* and *recommend,* the verb in the noun clause is always in the base form.
  It is <u>vital</u> that you **finish** the job by Friday.
  I <u>suggest</u> she **wear** a different dress to the party.

Exercise 2   **Identifying noun clauses**

A. **Underline the noun clause in each sentence. Circle the verb phrase in the main clause.**

1. It (is crucial) that companies provide health insurance benefits.
2. What they decided to do is ridiculous.
3. It is essential that you check the painting's authenticity.
4. We advise that you buy jewelry only from a reputable dealer.
5. The board demands that the school hire master teachers.
6. I don't agree with what he said.

B. **Look back at the student essay on page 98. Find four sentences with noun clauses. Then write the sentences below.**

1. _____

   _____

2. _____

   _____

3. _____

   _____

4. _____

   _____

Creating noun clauses

> Complete each unfinished sentence so that it has the same meaning as the statement printed above it. Use noun clauses with *that*.

1. The students want the college to add new math courses to the curricula.

   The students think _that the college should add new math courses to the_ _curricula._

2. The city residents want the mayor to lower the fare for public transportation.

   The city residents recommend _____

   _____

3. The community should provide after school programs for teenagers.

   Parents believe _____

   _____

4. The government must offer free health care for all citizens.

   It is crucial _____

   _____

5. Most employers want their workers to arrive on time.

   Most employers insist _____

   _____

Editing a paragraph

> Read the paragraph. Correct the mistakes in adverbial and noun clauses. There are six mistakes, including two punctuation mistakes.

> Identity theft occurs when someone steals your name, social security number, or credit card number and uses it for his/her own purposes. Although most people feel safe from identity theft thousands of people each year fall victim to this new form of crime. We recommend that you to protect yourself from this hideous crime. Do not disclose personal information (like your social security number) to strangers. Destroy all unused bank and credit card statements.

Keep an eye on your credit cards. Although credit cards make life easier you need to be cautious when using them. In case you become a victim of identity crime, follow these steps. We advise that you should file a police report as soon as you realize that something is wrong. It is crucial that you to notify your credit card companies and bank immediately. We also suggest that you could keep records of all your documents in a safe place. Therefore, if you become a victim, you will have all the necessary information to facilitate the filing process.

Exercise 5 Editing your first draft and rewriting

Review your essay for mistakes. Use the checklist. Then write a final draft.

Editor's Checklist

Put a check (✓) as appropriate.

- ☐ 1. Did you use adverbial clauses to show contrast and concession?
- ☐ 2. Did you remember to use a comma when the adverbial clause appears at the beginning of the sentence?
- ☐ 3. Did you use any noun clauses with *what* or *that*?
- ☐ 4. Did you remember to use the base form of the verb in noun clauses after certain noun adjectives and verbs?

In Part 5 you will . . .

- review the elements of argumentative writing.
- practice writing under a time limit.

Putting It All Together

In this part of the unit, you will complete five exercises to improve your accuracy, write a timed essay to improve your fluency, and explore topics for further writing.

Exercise 1   Identifying refutation and concession

Write *R* for each argument showing a refutation and *C* for each item showing concession.

_____ 1. Many people like the new technology of digital cameras. However, a number of artists like me feel that digital film is inferior to regular film.

_____ 2. Movie companies outside of the U.S. use American music recorded in the 1940s and 1950s but believe they should not have to pay for permission. This seems reasonable since this music has been around for such a long time.

_____ 3. Too many consumers think it is acceptable to use credit cards to buy more than they can afford. Unfortunately, if they continue to overspend year after year, they will become hopelessly in debt.

_____ 4. Even though some parents think it is a nuisance to put children between the ages of five and seven into special car seats, research has shown that this will save many lives.

_____ 5. The city maintains that a shopping mall on the waterfront is more valuable to the community than a park because it will create new jobs. As a member of the community, I would love to see a new park built there but realize that we really need the new jobs.

_____ 6. Large automobiles are popular in the United States, but they are using up our oil reserves, which are non-renewable. Therefore, only small cars should be produced.

Exercise 2   Using connectors to show additional information and show contrast

Combine the two sentences with a connector to indicate additional information or contrast. Check your punctuation carefully.

1. A lot of companies copy the ingredients found in famous perfumes. Other companies steal patterns for dishware, sheets, and towels.

_____

_____

2. Many college students know that plagiarism is illegal. Websites that sell essays continue to grow.

_____

_____

3. Writing a research paper takes time and patience. It takes determination.

_____

_____

4. Media related property theft has resulted in legal retaliation. The number of individuals illegally obtaining media online has increased.

_____

_____

5. Many consumers try to keep up with modern technology. This is almost impossible because what is popular today becomes obsolete tomorrow.

_____

_____

| Exercise 3 | **Using adverbial clauses to show contrast and concession** |

Add a main clause to the following adverbial clauses to create sentences that show contrast or concession. Check your punctuation carefully.

1. although people in the United States greet each other by shaking hands

_____

_____

2. while opponents say that television has a lot of violence

_____

_____

3. whereas many people go on vacation in the summer

_____

_____

4. although smoking has been proven to be a dangerous habit

_____

_____

5. even though cell phone users believe that they have the right to talk whenever they want

_____

_____

Creating noun clauses

Complete each unfinished sentence so that it has the same meaning as the statement printed above it. Use noun clauses with *that*.

1. Cyclists in the United States wear helmets.

   It is mandatory _____.

2. People are punished for stealing intellectual property.

   The government believes _____.

3. A driver should check the car's oil and tires before taking a long trip.

   It is essential _____.

4. The taxpayers want the mayor to build a new highway.

   The taxpayers propose _____.

5. College students should have their own computers.

   Colleges recommend _____.

Editing a paragraph

Read the paragraph and edit as necessary. There are nine mistakes.

To complete a research project on the Internet, it is important that you must find a good search engine. There are many available some are better than others. Once you have chosen your search engine, it is essential that you should narrow your search to a specific topic. Type in the key words for your search. We recommend that you will check your spelling carefully. If you misspell too many words, you will not get the right results. As soon as you have your list of websites, we suggest that you quickly to scan the list. Some people choose websites randomly, others find that the first five to ten are usually the best. Be prepared to look at a lot of websites before you find what you need. Open the sites and skim them to find out if the information will work for your project. It is tempting to copy the material that you have found, it is mandatory that you to use your own words when you write your paper. You should include the website address in your final report.

TIMED WRITING: 60 minutes

Write a five-paragraph essay on whether or not you think new technology such as cell phones, computers, and DVDs benefit our society. Before you begin to write, review the suggested time management strategy below.

Step 1 **BRAINSTORMING: 5 minutes**

Write down ideas and vocabulary for your essay on a separate piece of paper. List three reasons that support your position. Then list as many details as you can to explain each reason.

Step 2 **OUTLINING: 5 minutes**

Write an outline for your essay in the form below.

Introduction

Hook: _____

_____

_____

Background information: _____

_____

_____

Thesis statement: _____

_____

_____

reason 1 **Body Paragraph 1**

Topic sentence: _____

_____

_____

Supporting details: _____

_____

_____

reason 2 **Body Paragraph 2**

Topic sentence: _____

_____

_____

Supporting details: _____

_____

_____

reason 3 | **Body Paragraph 3**

Topic sentence: _____

_____

_____

Supporting details: _____

_____

_____

Conclusion

Restatement: _____

_____

_____

Prediction, warning, or issue in broader context: _____

_____

_____

Step 3 | **WRITING: 40 minutes**

Use your brainstorming notes and outline to write your first draft on a
separate piece of paper.

Step 4 | **EDITING: 10 minutes**

When you have finished your first draft, check it for mistakes, using the
checklist below.

Editor's Checklist

Put a check (✓) as appropriate.

☐ 1. Do you have a thesis statement that takes a clear position?

☐ 2. Do the body paragraphs include distinct reasons to support your
position?

☐ 3. Does the third body paragraph contain a counter-argument with either
a refutation or a concession?

☐ 4. Did you use connectors that show contrast or addition?

☐ 5. Did you use any noun clauses?

☐ 6. Did you use adverbial clauses?

☐ 7. Does your conclusion repeat the reasons in your argument?

1. **Write a five-paragraph argumentative essay on one of the following topics.**

   - In some countries, people have boycotted fast food chains because they feel that they pose a threat to the national character of their cities. Write an essay in which you either support or oppose the growth of fast food chains around the world.
   - In America, adopted children can now find out the identity of their birth parents. Write an essay in which you explain whether this is a good or bad idea.
   - In some countries, voting in national elections is mandatory, but in the U.S. there are no laws forcing people to vote. Discuss why voting should or should not be mandatory.
   - Despite the many timesaving devices in our homes, people today are working harder and longer. Explain whether it would it be better for people to work less and have more leisure time.

2. **Write a five-paragraph argumentative essay on one of the topics above, but from a friend's point of view. Interview a friend, classmate, or relative about his or her views on the topic. Take notes during the interview to use for your essay.**

3. **Use the Internet or other sources to research one of the topics or a topic of your choice. Then write an argumentative essay based upon your research.**

Unit 5

Classification Essays

Unit Goals

Rhetorical focus:
- classification organization
- organizing principles of importance and chronology

Language focus:
- gerunds and infinitives
- sentence patterns with verbs

PART 1

Stimulating Ideas

The jobs of the future will demand certain abilities from the new work force. In this unit you will write about the talents and skills you possess that will make you competitive in the marketplace.

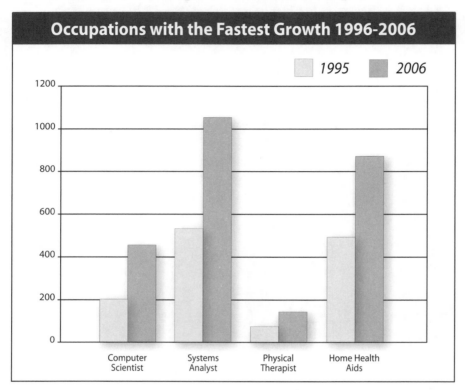

Occupations with the Fastest Growth 1996-2006

1995   2006

Exercise 1   Thinking about the topic

A. Discuss the graph with a partner.

- What occupation has experienced the fastest growth? What do you think is causing this growth?
- Compared to 1996, approximately how many more jobs were there in the field of computer science in 2006?
- Why do you think the home health aid field experienced so much growth?

B. Make notes about jobs that interest you. Then discuss in small groups.

Exercise 2   Reading about the topic

The authors of this text report on the skills employers are looking for in new employees.

Skills for Jobs of the Future

Are you a college student planning to enter the workforce? Or are you a worker hoping to advance in your field? A new **survey** shows that you will need job training and education beyond what many job applicants have.

Workers who possess critical skills are needed to fill thousands of new jobs. The desired skills are in two categories: essential and technical. The essential skills include team building, communication, customer service, and problem solving. The technical skills required are math and writing, as well as knowledge of computer applications, such as e-mail systems, Microsoft® Word, Excel and Access.

The study, Skills 2006, was based on a survey of 153 small, medium, and large employers. Fifty-six percent of the companies responding to the survey said their **applicant pools** did not possess the desired skills. Another 42 percent of the companies **surveyed** felt their current workforce **lacked** critical skills. Don Jackson, human resources director at Procter & Gamble in Iowa City, said the skills required for employment have increased as companies have changed the way they hire workers. "In the past, we were willing to take high school graduates and do the training ourselves," Jackson said. "In the future, we really need to get applicants with technical training." He stated that many technical colleges were more efficient at providing the kind of training needed than the companies themselves.

Another study found that many employers required a minimum of a two-year degree or technical certification. That study also showed that in the near future 50 percent of the new jobs will require a four-year or graduate degree. "Right now, 25 percent of our existing labor force has a baccalaureate (four-year) degree," said Norm Nielsen, president of Kirkwood Community College. "If 50 percent of the new jobs are going to require a four-year or graduate degree, we are facing a real challenge." Employers also mentioned a particular **shortage** of women and minority applicants with training in technical programs.

If you want to be competitive in the job market, you should be developing either essential or technical skills to **ensure** your success in the future.

---

survey: study
applicant pools: supply of potential employees
surveyed: questioned

lacked: were missing
shortage: low number
ensure: make certain

Understanding the text

Write *T* for true or *F* for false for each statement.

_____ 1. Most applicants today do not have the skills needed for jobs.

_____ 2. Problem solving and knowledge of computer applications are both essential skills.

_____ 3. The majority of companies report that hiring practices have remained the same.

_____ 4. More men than women are making advances in the technical fields.

_____ 5. It is only necessary to get a two-year degree to be competitive in the future job market.

Exercise 4 **Responding to the text**

Write your answers for each question in complete sentences. Then discuss your answers with a partner.

1. Which groups of people need to be concerned about increasing their skills?

    _____

    _____

    _____

    _____

2. What are some of the computer skills needed for the future?

    _____

    _____

    _____

    _____

3. What is "Skills 2006?"

    _____

    _____

    _____

    _____

4. How have hiring practices changed in many companies?

    _____

    _____

    _____

    _____

5. Why is it a problem that a larger percentage of the new jobs will require at least a four-year degree?

_____

_____

_____

_____

Exercise 5 Freewriting

Write for ten to fifteen minutes about the topic below. Express yourself as well as you can. Don't worry about mistakes.

The jobs of the future will require technical and other important abilities. What kinds of abilities do you possess for a potential career?

- What are some of your specific skills and talents? Describe them.
- How did you develop these skills and talents?

In Part 2 you will . . .

- learn how to organize a classification essay.
- brainstorm ideas and specific vocabulary to use in your writing.
- create an outline for a classification essay.

PART 2

Brainstorming and Outlining

✎ WRITING TASK

In this unit, you will write a five-paragraph classification essay about the abilities that will help you succeed in the career of your choice.

Exercise 1   Brainstorming ideas

Fill in the chart below with the names of three professions that interest you. Next to each profession write the abilities you possess for that profession. Look at the example before you begin.

Profession	Abilities
history teacher	*confidence*

Exercise 2   Brainstorming vocabulary

A. Classify your abilities from Exercise 1 by using the chart below. Can you add additional abilities to the chart?

leadership	problem-solving	creativity	interpersonal skills	knowledge
confidence				

B. Use the chart in part A to help you present your abilities to a small group.

Rhetorical Focus

Classification Organization

In a classification essay, information is organized into meaningful categories or groups and each follows a single, unifying principle.

The Introduction
- The hook introduces the information to be classified.
- Background information includes a general statement or statements that give a broader picture of the subject matter to be discussed.
- The thesis statement contains the topic and the controlling idea for the whole essay. It tells what is being classified and how it is being organized.

The Body
- The topic sentence clearly describes the category or group in each paragraph. It supports and expands the thesis statement and the controlling idea that are stated in the introduction. The topic sentence is often the first sentence of the paragraph.
- One category or group is described in each paragraph. The information in each paragraph is ordered logically, for example in order of importance or in chronological order.
- The supporting details can be descriptions, definitions, examples, anecdotes, statistics, or quotations that elaborate on the topic sentence.
- The concluding sentence may either bring the idea of the paragraph to a close or suggest the content of the next paragraph.

The Conclusion
- It restates the content of each paragraph.
- It may make a prediction, give advice or make a general statement.

Exercise 3   **Reading a student essay**

Read the essay. What kinds of computer programs are discussed in the essay?

Graphic Design Programs

Graphic design has become an essential tool in desktop publishing. Only a short time ago, people relied on professionals to perform tasks that the computer has now made possible for anyone who takes the time to learn them. Graphic design programs are classified according to their function.

Dreamweaver and Flash MX are two of the most well-known programs used to develop a web page. Dreamweaver is in an HTML format, which is one of the languages used to create simple web pages. This type of web page program allows for a navigation bar, some pictures in the background, and uncomplicated animations. With Flash MX, you can develop very dynamic web pages. For example, you can have transitional pages, which are links that guide you from one slide (or portion of the slide) to another. You can also have animated introductions and create diverse effects with the buttons at the bottom of the pages.

If you are looking for programs that can design flyers, posters, and cards, Photoshop and Illustrator are very useful programs. Photoshop lets you create whatever you want, from websites and posters to catalogs and business cards. With this program, you can repair or enhance any part of an old photograph by making the image brighter or adding shadow. Illustrator is very similar to Photoshop, but Illustrator is especially good for making flyers, business cards, CD covers, and magazine layouts. It is very useful for designing logos and even creating new styles of fonts.

Swift 3D and Swish are animation programs that can be used to produce a 2- or 3-dimensional style, depending on the effect desired. Two-dimensional animations do not have depth, but are flat planes like pieces of paper. Three-dimensional animations have depth, as in real life when you see a box from a distance. These programs allow you to create something as simple as a 3-dimensional sphere to something as complex as a house or a car. Swish also provides more options for font design than Flash MX.

All these programs can be used together to create a dynamic web page. Three-dimensional animations have depth, as in real life when you see a box from a distance. Dreamweaver can be used as the base program to make the "skeleton" of the web page. The others can flesh it out. Flash makes the pages dynamic. Photoshop helps with the creation of photos: Illustrator and Swift make it possible to create company logos in either 2- or 3-dimensions, and Swish helps with the effects on the font design. In the world of graphics, you have to be up-to-date with the latest programs to improve your skills as well as give your clients the best.

Exercise 4   **Examining the student essay**

A. Respond to the essay by answering the questions below in complete sentences.

1. What is an advantage of using the Flash MX program? _____

_____

_____

2. Compared to Illustrator, what special feature does Photoshop have? _____

_____

_____

3. What is the major difference between Swish and Flash MX? _____

_____

_____

4. What is the difference between a 2- and 3- dimensional animation? _____

_____

_____

5. Have you used any of the graphic design programs discussed in the student essay? If so, what did you use if for, and did you find it user-friendly?

_____

_____

_____

B. Examine the organization of the essay on pages 121–123 by answering the questions below. Then compare your answers with a partner.

1. Circle the sentence(s) that make up the hook.

2. Underline the thesis statement. Rewrite it in your own words. _____
   _____
   _____

3. According to what principle are the categories being grouped? _____
   _____
   _____

4. What is the category for body paragraph 1? _____
   _____

5. What is the category for body paragraph 2? _____
   _____

6. What is the category for body paragraph 3? _____
   _____

7. The writer concludes his essay with

   a. a prediction.   b. advice.   c. a general statement.

Exercise 5 **Writing an outline**

Review your brainstorming ideas and your freewriting exercise. Then use the chart below to write an outline for an essay about the abilities that will help you succeed in the profession of your choice.

Introduction

Hook: _____
_____
_____

Background information: _____
_____
_____

Thesis statement: _____
_____
_____

Body Paragraph 1

Category 1: _____

_____

_____

Supporting details: _____

_____

_____

Body Paragraph 2

Category 2: _____

_____

_____

Supporting details: _____

_____

_____

Body Paragraph 3

Category 3: _____

_____

_____

Supporting details: _____

_____

_____

Conclusion

Restatement: _____

_____

_____

Prediction, advice, or statement: _____

_____

_____

In Part 3 you will . . .

- learn about the organizing principles of importance and chronology.
- write a first draft of your classification essay.

Read the essay. According to the writer, what will be the fastest growing careers?

The Fastest Growing Careers

Where will the jobs of the future be? Many students who are not certain about their career path may be asking this question. If you already know what field you want to work in, you might want to stick to your plan. However, if you are one of the many students who are still confused about which career to pursue, here are the jobs that will have the most growth in the number of people employed over the next decade.

The highest percentage of growth will be among computer scientists, computer engineers, computer support specialists, and systems analysts. These are the best career opportunities for people with a bachelor's or master's degree in engineering or science. On the average, these occupational categories will grow by 106 percent. Personality types most suitable for these professions are those that are investigative in nature. These occupations often involve working with ideas and require a lot of time thinking. They require people to search for facts and figure out problems.

The second-highest percentage of growth will take place among database administrators and desktop publishing specialists. These are highly desirable and attractive career options for people with a bachelor's or master's in business administration. In addition, people who have special artistic talents and enjoy working with computers will find these professions very rewarding. The average growth rate in these occupational categories in the next ten years will be 75 percent.

The third-highest growth rate will be among personal care home health aides and human service workers with associate's degrees (two-year degrees). As the United States population continues to grow older over the next decade, this field will increase by 55 percent. Within these groups, the highest-paid jobs for people with an associate's degree will be respiratory therapists, cardiovascular technologists, and nuclear medicine technologists, with average growth rates of around 31 percent. For each of these jobs, employers expect applicants to have a strong background in science and mathematics. Those in personal care and human service occupations should be able to listen to and understand verbal information and, most importantly, they should be able to communicate written information and medical instructions to their clients.

In summary, the fastest growing careers for the 21st century will be in occupational areas related to computer science and health and human services. We live in an information age where speed and knowledge, as well as interpersonal relationships and the ability to provide needed human services, are the essence of life. All these occupations and skills represent the vital force or energy that drives the economy.

| Exercise 2 | **Analyzing the student essay**

A. Respond to the essay by answering the questions below in full sentences.

1. What are some of the essential skills computer engineers and scientists need? _____

_____

_____

2. How do careers in database administration and desktop publishing rank in terms of jobs of the future? _____

_____

_____

3. Who are the highest-paid professionals within the associate's degree category? _____

_____

_____

4. What are the top skills needed to become a human service professional?

_____

_____

_____

5. According to the writer, what forces will drive the economy in the 21st century? _____

_____

_____

6. Do any of the jobs discussed in the student essay match your abilities? Explain why. _____

_____

_____

B. Examine the organization of the essay on pages 126–127. Then answer the questions below. Compare your answers with a partner.

1. Rewrite the hook in your own words. _____

_____

2. Underline the thesis statement. Rewrite it in your own words. _____

_____

3. In what kind of order is the information presented? _____

_____

4. What phrases in the three body paragraphs illustrate this order? _____

_____

5. What kind of supporting details does the writer use in body paragraph 3?

_____

_____

Language Focus

Classification of Groups

When writing a classification essay, you should establish meaningful and logical categories using similar characteristics, qualities, or functions. The groupings should also share a single underlying principle in order to preserve unity.

For example, one principle of classification for archivists, publishers, and librarians is *people who work with books*. Archivists, publishers, and librarians all belong to that group.

Exercise 3   **Classifying with groups**

Select the occupations from the box to create three specific groups with common characteristics. Then write the principle of classification for each group.

park ranger	interpreter	civil engineer
linguist	landscaper	surveyor
architect	farmer	speech therapist

1. Group 1: _____

   _____

   _____

   Principle of classification: _____

2. Group 2: _____

   _____

   _____

   Principle of classification: _____

3. Group 3: _____

   _____

   _____

   Principle of classification: _____

Establishing the Order of Importance, Degree, and Size

Once you have created logical categories for your classification essay, you will need to organize the information in a logical order. Arranging facts in order of importance, degree or size will help you establish useful hierarchies. Compare the two examples below.

example 1 — An important skill to succeed in teaching is the ability to communicate ideas. Another important skill is the ability to break down information. Computer skills are also important.

example 2 — **The most important** skill needed to succeed in teaching is the ability to break down information. **The second most important** skill is the ability to communicate ideas. Computer skills are useful but are **the least important** ability needed to be a teacher.

In the first example, the information is presented in no particular order. However, in the second example, the writer uses a range of expressions to organize the ideas in order of importance. As a result, the second example shows greater clarity and coherence.

- The following expressions will help you rank objects or ideas in order of importance, degree or size:

the most/greatest	the second most/greatest	the least/fewest
the fastest	the second fastest	the slowest
the best	the next best	the worst
the highest	the second highest	the lowest
the largest	the second largest	the smallest
the maximum		the minimum
the most significant		the least significant
the most important		the least important

The highest percentage of the total number of teachers work in elementary schools. **The second highest** amount teach in junior high schools and high schools. **The smallest** number of teachers work in adult education.

- To show similarity or equality, use *the same, almost the same,* and *similar to.*

The skills needed to succeed in some professions are **the same**.
The artistic abilities of fine artists are **similar to** those of photographers.

Using expressions that show importance or similarity

Study the graph about working hours in different countries. Then complete the sentences with the phrases from the box below.

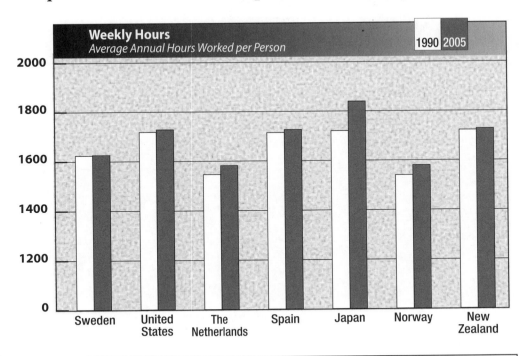

| the fewest   the same   almost the same   the smallest   the greatest |

1. In 2005 Japan had _____ number of working hours.

2. In 1990 Spain and Japan had _____ number of working hours.

3. People in the Netherlands and Norway spent _____ number of hours working.

4. The United States and Spain had _____ number of working hours in 2005.

5. The countries that had _____ amount of change between 1990 and 2005 were Sweden and New Zealand.

Writing a first draft

Review your outline. Then write your first draft of a five-paragraph classification essay about abilities you possess for your potential career.

Peer editing a first draft

After you write your first draft, exchange it with a partner. Answer the questions on the checklist on page 132. Write comments or questions for your partner's draft. Then read your partner's comments about your first draft and revise it as necessary.

Editor's Checklist

Put a check (✓) as appropriate. Write answers in complete sentences on the lines provided.

☐ 1. Does the introduction include background information about the topic? Write the background information here. _____

_____

☐ 2. Does the thesis statement have a unifying principle? Write the unifying principle. _____

_____

☐ 3. Does each body paragraph include a distinct category? Write the categories here for each paragraph. _____

_____

☐ 4. Are the supporting details for each paragraph sufficient?

☐ 5. Does the conclusion restate the three categories?

☐ 6. Is there advice, a prediction, or a general statement in the conclusion? If not, make a suggestion to the writer about how to revise. _____

_____

_____

In Part 4 you will . . .

- learn about gerunds and infinitives.
- study sentence patterns with verbs.
- edit your first draft.

PART 4

Editing Your Writing

Now that you have written your first draft, it is time to edit. Editing involves making changes to your writing to improve it and correct mistakes.

Language Focus

Gerunds

A gerund is an *-ing* form of a verb. It can be used in a sentence to name an activity or a situation.

- A gerund can be one word (*eating*). It can also be part of a longer phrase with an adverb (*eating quickly*), with a noun (*eating dinner*), or with a prepositional phrase (*eating in a restaurant*).

- All verbs, except modal verbs, have gerund forms.

Gerunds Following Verbs

- A gerund can act as the subject of a sentence.
  Eating dinner by candlelight is romantic.

- A gerund can also follow a verb. Some common verbs that can be followed by gerunds are *enjoy, consider, like, dislike, practice, prefer,* and *recommend*.
  I <u>like</u> **eating dinner** late.

Gerunds Following Prepositions

- Gerunds can follow prepositions such as *about, for, on,* or *in*.

- One common pattern of gerunds following prepositions is *be* + adjective + preposition + gerund. Some examples of this pattern include *be concerned about, be involved in, be good at, be responsible for, be accustomed to, be interested in,* and *be nervous about*.
  I <u>am interested in</u> **acquiring** new skills.

Exercise 1 Identifying gerunds

Underline the gerunds in the following sentences. Write _S_ if the gerund is the subject or _V_ if it follows the verb.

_S_ 1. <u>Piloting</u> a plane involves good judgment.

____ 2. Nutritionists suggest eating fresh fruits and vegetables.

____ 3. In addition to talent, being a professional musician demands commitment.

____ 4. Radiology technicians practice taking x-rays.

____ 5. Learning a foreign language is rewarding.

____ 6. For many college students, studying abroad can be an interesting experience.

Exercise 2 Using gerunds in sentences

Complete each sentence with a gerund. Compare your answers with a partner.

1. We discussed <u>changing the schedule</u>_____.

2. I always enjoy _____.

3. _____ can be a wonderful experience.

4. Many people dislike _____.

5. _____ is a useful skill to learn.

6. If you want to feel better, you should avoid _____.

Exercise 3 Using gerunds after prepositions

Complete the following sentences with the gerund form of the verbs in the box.

> memorize   discover   ~~predict~~   take   improve   research

1. Meteorologists are responsible for _____<u>predicting</u>_____ the weather.

2. Politicians are often concerned about _____ the community.

3. Actors are good at _____ their scripts.

4. Historians are accustomed to _____ the lives of world leaders.

5. Astronomers are interested in _____ new galaxies.

6. Students are nervous about _____ exams.

Exercise 4 Forming sentences with prepositions and gerunds

Write sentences about yourself using the phrase in parentheses and a gerund. Compare your answers with a partner.

1. (be accustomed to) <u>I am accustomed to staying up late.</u>

2. (be interested in) _____

3. (be nervous about) _____

4. (be responsible for) _____

5. (be concerned about) _____

6. (be involved in) _____

Language Focus

Infinitives

An infinitive is formed with *to* + the base form of the verb. An infinitive can be used in place of a noun to describe an activity expressed by a verb.

- An infinitive can be part of a longer phrase with an adverb (*to drive quickly*) or a noun (*to drive a car*).

- All verbs, except modal verbs, have an infinitive form.

Infinitives After Verbs

An infinitive can follow a verb or the object of a verb. In some cases the object of a verb can be omitted.

- Verbs that follow the verb + infinitive pattern include *agree, appear, decide, learn, like, plan,* and *seem*.

  I <u>like</u> **to eat** out on Saturday nights.

- Verbs that follow the verb + object + infinitive pattern include *advise, allow, cause, get, hire, invite, order, require, teach,* and *tell*.

  The counselor <u>advised</u> Thomas **to take** a Biology class.

- Verbs that follow the verb + (object) + infinitive pattern include *ask, choose, expect, need* and *want*.

  I <u>want</u> **to go** home.

  I <u>want</u> you **to go** home.

Writing sentences with infinitives

Rearrange the words and phrases below to make complete sentences.

1. arrive / the principal / to / on time / the teachers / expected

   _____

2. new employees / to / is planning / hire / the company

   _____

3. to / next year / graduate / expects / Barbara

   _____

4. to / require / their medical exams / all hospitals / pass / doctors

   _____

5. a foreign language / we / to / learn / decided

   _____

6. dress appropriately / job applicants / employment agencies / to / for their interviews / advise

   _____

Exercise 6 **Completing sentences with infinitives**

Complete each sentence with an infinitive. Remember to use an object where needed. Compare your answers with a partner.

1. The professor agreed _____ .
2. The policeman asked _____ .
3. My doctor advised _____ .
4. The mayor needs _____ .
5. My best friend wants _____ .
6. Many children learn _____ .

Language Focus

Verbs Following *Make, Let,* and *Have*

The verbs *make, have,* and *let* are followed by an object and the base form of a verb, not the infinitive. The objects of these verbs perform the action expressed by the base form.

She **made** her son <u>clean</u> his room.
She made her son to clean his room. (INCORRECT).

Using make, have and let

Complete the following sentences using *make, have,* or *let* and a base form.

1. The principal of the high school <u>had the students attend an assembly</u> .

2. My parents _____ .

3. The lifeguard _____ .

4. The judge _____ .

5. The bus driver _____ .

6. The airlines _____ .

Editing the paragraph

Read the paragraph. Correct the mistakes in gerund and infinitive forms. There are seven mistakes.

Find the right career may seem like an overwhelming task for many. If you are looking for job opportunities, you need take enough time to explore all the options. Begin by assess your skills. Decide what you are good at doing and what you enjoy. Are you interested in designing or creating things with your hands? Perhaps you are more accustomed to sit at a computer. Do you like working indoors, or do you enjoy be outside in nature? Some people prefer work on a team, while others dislike working with others. This may be the most important decision you will ever make, so explore your talents and abilities carefully, and do not let anyone to influence you.

Review your essay for mistakes. Use the checklist below. Then write a final draft.

Editor's Checklist

Put a check (✓) as appropriate.

☐ 1. Does the essay have any gerunds as subjects?

☐ 2. Does the essay have any gerunds following a verb?

☐ 3. Did you use any gerunds following prepositions?

☐ 4. Did you use any infinitives following objects?

☐ 5. Did you use the correct word pattern for the verbs *make*, *let*, and *have*?

In Part 5 you will . . .

- review the elements of a classification essay.
- practice writing under a time limit.

Putting It All Together

In this part of the unit, you will complete six exercises to improve your accuracy, write a timed essay to improve your fluency, and explore topics for further writing.

Exercise 1 — Using verbs followed by gerunds

Complete the following sentences with a gerund form of one of the words in the box.

form	arrive	practice	write	prepare	receive

1. Chefs enjoy _____ unusual meals.

2. The heads of state considered _____ an alliance.

3. Bankers dislike _____ complaints from their customers.

4. _____ at the airport two hours before departure is recommended.

5. Many authors prefer _____ directly on a computer rather than with pen and paper.

6. _____ many times before performing helps musicians.

Exercise 2 — Choosing the correct preposition

Write the correct preposition from the box to follow the adjective in each sentence.

for	in	to	about	at	with

1. Doctors are accustomed _____ working long hours.

2. Lawyers are good _____ arguing a case.

3. Archeologists are interested _____ digging for fossils.

4. Police are responsible _____ protecting the community.

5. Conservationists are concerned _____ saving our forests and waterways.

6. Investors are nervous _____ losing their money.

Choosing the correct verb

Choose the correct verb to complete the following sentences.

1. My professor _____ me to take a writing course.
   a. let
   b. advised
   c. made

2. My boss _____ me to leave early.
   a. allowed
   b made
   c. had

3. The librarian _____ the children to be quiet.
   a. let
   b. had
   c. expected

4. The director _____ the actor repeat the scene.
   a. had
   b. asked
   c. told

5. The baseball coach _____ the team play an extra game.
   a. wanted
   b. expected
   c. let

6. The car mechanic _____ an assistant to help repair the engines.
   a. made
   b. had
   c. hired

Using the base form or the infinitive form

Circle the correct form of the verb in the parentheses.

1. The pilot had the passengers (fasten / to fasten) their seatbelts.

2. The security guards did not allow anyone (enter / to enter) the building without identification.

3. The driving instructor did not let his pupil (drive / to drive) on the highway.

4. The chairman of the board did not expect his entire staff (attend / to attend) the meeting.

5. The law firm made the paralegals (work / to work) overtime.

6. The student did not want his classmates (read / to read) his paper.

Classifying with groups

Select words from the box to create three specific groups. Then give the principle of classification for each group.

Africa	Japan	Thailand
Vietnam	Italy	Europe
Switzerland	Asia	France

1. Group 1: _____

   _____

   _____

   Principle of classification: _____

2. Group 2: _____

   _____

   _____

   Principle of classification: _____

3. Group 3: _____

   _____

   _____

   Principle of classification: _____

Editing a Paragraph

Read the paragraph and edit as necessary. There are eight mistakes.

There are many good reasons for taking a temporary position. For college students who are interested in enter the workforce, a temporary position can be very beneficial. If young people are concerned about choose the wrong profession, career counselors advise them get experience in a variety of fields. They recommend to working in a company on a temporary basis to determine if the job is suitable. Today companies receive hundreds of resumes for one job opening. Therefore, potential workers need to be good at communicate, writing, and problem solving in order to compete. A temp job allows someone to learn the necessary skills needed to obtain a better position in the future. It may even help to impress potential employers. Companies expect employees to applying themselves and sharpen their skills. Job seekers need to show how valuable they are if they want get hired. While working as a temporary employee, they can prove themselves on the job and let the company to know they are ready for a full-time position.

TIMED WRITING: 60 minutes

Write a five-paragraph essay in which you classify the types of entertainment you like the most.

Step 1 BRAINSTORMING: 5 minutes

Write down ideas and vocabulary for your brainstorm on a separate piece of paper. You may want to use a chart similar to the one on page 120.

Step 2 OUTLINING: 5 minutes

Write an outline for your essay in the form below.

Introduction

Hook: _____

_____

_____

Background information: _____

_____

_____

Thesis statement: _____

_____

_____

Body Paragraph 1

Category 1: _____

_____

_____

Supporting details: _____

_____

_____

_____

_____

Body Paragraph 2

Category 2: _____

_____

_____

Supporting details: _____

_____

_____

_____

_____

Body Paragraph 3

Category 3: _____

_____

_____

Supporting details: _____

_____

_____

_____

_____

Conclusion

Restatement: _____

_____

_____

Prediction, advice, or statement: _____

_____

_____

_____

_____

Step 3 | **WRITING: 40 minutes**

Use your brainstorming notes and outline to write your first draft on a separate piece of paper.

Step 4 | **EDITING: 10 minutes**

When you have finished your first draft, check it for mistakes using the checklist on page 144.

Editor's Checklist

Put a check (✓) as appropriate.

☐ 1. Does the introduction tell what is being classified?

☐ 2. Does each body paragraph explain a different category?

☐ 3. Are the categories arranged according to one unifying principle?

☐ 4. Does the conclusion restate the three categories?

☐ 5. Does the essay have any gerunds as subjects or following the verb?

☐ 6. Did you use any gerunds following prepositions?

☐ 7. Did you use any infinitives following objects?

☐ 8. Did you use the correct word pattern for verbs make, let and have?

Topics for Future Writing

Write a five-paragraph classification essay on one of the following topics.

- What are the advantages of different modes of transportation? For the unifying principle you may consider: land, water, and air; transportation in cities; transportation in the country.
- How would you categorize options for vacation planning?
- Categorize food according to its nutritional benefits.
- Classify the types of friends you have.
- Use the Internet to research one of the following topics:
   ecosystems (desert, rainforest, tropical)
   environmental pollution (air, water, soil)
   types of animals (birds, mammals, reptiles)
   types of carbohydrates (fruits, vegetables, starches)

Unit 6

Reaction Essays

Unit Goals

Rhetorical focus:
- reaction organization

Language focus:
- prepositional phrases
- similes
- restrictive and nonrestrictive relative clauses

PART 1

Stimulating Ideas

A good photograph elicits a strong reaction from the viewer. In this unit you will describe your reaction to two photographs.

"Playing in Street Sprinkler"

"Children Playing Baseball"

Exercise 1   Thinking about the topic

A. Discuss the pictures with a partner.

- What is happening in these pictures?
- How are the children reacting to the experience?
- Can you remember a similar experience? How did you feel?

B. Make notes about what makes an individual photograph memorable to you. Then discuss in small groups.

Exercise 2   Reading about the topic

Not every photograph is a work of art, but everyone can learn the concepts of good picture-taking. This article discusses some important principles of creative photography.

Creative Photography

Photography, like all forms of visual art, does not have rules. However, the composition, which is the arrangement of the elements in a photograph, does. Composition has a number of guidelines that can be understood, considered, and applied. Successful pictures are usually simple pictures. This means that the message is unambiguous, or clear. Distractions have been eliminated in order to let the main subject **dominate.**

It is **vitally** important for a good photograph to have a main center of interest. This main center of interest can be large or small in the frame, but as long as it contrasts with its surroundings, it will demand attention. All other elements in photographs are secondary when compared to this main center of interest.

Contrast itself is very important. It appears in many shapes, textures, and forms: straight and curved, **rough** and smooth, light and dark, large and small, near and far, sharp and out of focus. Also, different colors contrast or **harmonize** with each other. Balancing the contrast is another factor to take into account. It can be viewed in terms of shapes, colors or **tones.** The feeling of the overall composition of the photograph is what is most important. In general, the rule for contrast is if it feels right, then it is right.

Lines play an important part in the design of photos. Lines can **dictate** the way in which we view photos. Ideally they can lead the eye to the main center of interest. The positioning within the frame of this center of interest influences the **mood** of the photograph. Placing a subject centrally can create a peaceful, evenly balanced feeling. A subject placed nearer an edge, corner, or the periphery takes on a more dynamic role in the frame. The photographer must decide what is appropriate for each subject and scene.

Viewpoint is another important factor. Photographers should resist taking all their shots (pictures) at standing eye level. It is essential to study a subject from different points of view or positions. It's surprising how a change in viewpoint can also result in different lighting effects. As a result, a range of pictures can result from such a simple action.

dominate: stand out
vitally: extremely
contrast: comparison between two things or people
rough: uneven

harmonize: complement
tones: shades of color
dictate: influence
mood: feeling

The purpose of art is to create an image which brings about an emotional response. The most important part of any visual art, including photography, is the message, or what is communicated to the viewer. The storytelling element of the picture is vital if it is to be appreciated by others. Even though a photograph may be technically excellent, if it communicates nothing, it will not be a success.

Leo Palmer APSA, Northumberland, UK

Exercise 3 Understanding the text

Write *T* for true or *F* for false for each statement.

_____ 1. A great picture is always complex.

_____ 2. A main center of interest is usually large.

_____ 3. Rough and smooth are examples of balance.

_____ 4. Lines help the viewer focus on the main center of interest.

_____ 5. It is important to consider lighting when the viewpoint is moved.

Exercise 4 Responding to the text

Write your answers for each question in full sentences. Then discuss your answers with a partner.

1. What is an important difference between photography and the composition of a photograph? _____

_____

2. What makes the center of interest stand out? _____

_____

3. What are three different types of contrast? _____

_____

4. How can a change in viewpoint affect a photograph? _____

_____

5. How do you approach taking a photograph? Do you have any special techniques? _____

_____

Freewriting

Write for ten to fifteen minutes about the topic below. Express yourself as well as you can. Don't worry about mistakes.

Go back and look at the two photographs, "Playing in Street Sprinkler" and "Children Playing Baseball" in relation to what you learned in the essay "Creative Photography."

- What is alike and different in the two photos?
- What kind of emotional responses do the photos evoke?

In Part 2 you will . . .

- learn about reaction organization.
- brainstorm ideas and specific vocabulary to use in your writing.
- create an outline for your essay.

PART 2

Brainstorming and Outlining

✍ **WRITING TASK**

In this unit, you will write a five-paragraph reaction essay in response to the two photographs on page 146.

Exercise 1   **Brainstorming ideas**

A. Match the terms with the correct definition.

Terms	Definitions
_____ 1. periphery	a. quality that makes a surface look smooth or rough
_____ 2. foreground	b. point the viewer focuses on
_____ 3. background	c. part of the photo that appears closest
_____ 4. texture	d. part of the photo that appears the furthest away
_____ 5. shape	f. two dimensional form of an object or person
_____ 6. main center of interest	g. the outer edge of an area

B. Look at the photographs on page 146. Describe the elements of each photograph using adjectives from the box below.

> **Adjectives of shape and texture**
> **Shape:** round, rectangular, conical, ~~umbrella-like~~, square, oval, arched, semicircular, elliptical, triangular, straight, curved
> **Texture:** smooth, ~~shiny~~, rough, furry, uneven, rocky, bumpy, irregular, wavy, jagged, flaky, cracked, raised, fuzzy, sandy

Elements	"Playing in Street Sprinkler"	"Children Playing Baseball"
Main center of interest	shiny, umbrella-like fountain	
Foreground		
Background		

Brainstorming vocabulary

A. Select adjectives from the list below or other adjectives that you know to describe the mood of the two photographs. You may use an adjective more than once.

delicate	light	serious	nostalgic	mysterious	solemn
playful	active	carefree	gentle	soothing	competitive
lazy	sterile	fun	noble	lonely	mellow
friendly	refreshing	peaceful			

"Children Playing Baseball"   **"Playing in the Street Sprinkler"**

_____   _____

_____   _____

_____   _____

_____   _____

_____   _____

B. On a separate piece of paper, write three sentences that describe the mood of each photograph. Use adjectives from the lists you created above. You may use more than one adjective in each sentence.

Rhetorical Focus

Reaction Organization

In a reaction essay, the writer analyzes and evaluates his response to a prompt or prompts, which may be written works or images.

Introduction
- The hook focuses the reader's attention on the subject matter discussed in the essay.
- Background information includes the title, the name of the writer, artist or photographer, the date of the work, or other general information.
- The thesis statement may describe the message or the mood of the prompt(s). When more than one prompt is discussed, the thesis may make a general comparison between the two written works or images.

Body Paragraphs 1 and 2
- The topic sentence in each paragraph talks about one aspect of the message of the prompt.

- One aspect of the prompt is described in each paragraph in terms of whatever applies. In the case of a photograph, it could be the main center of interest, the positioning of objects and people, the contrast, lines, lighting, viewpoint, or mood.
- The paragraphs analyze what the written work or image is trying to convey—what message it carries.
- Each paragraph gives evidence to support its analysis.

Body Paragraph 3
- The topic sentence summarizes the similarities and differences between the prompts.
- This paragraph can explain the similarities and differences between two prompts.

Conclusion
- The conclusion restates the thesis. It may also summarize the similarities and differences discussed in body paragraph 3.
- It draws conclusions about the writer's reaction to the prompt(s).

Exercise 3 **Reading a student essay**

Look at the images. Then read the essay on page 153. How does the writer interpret the emotions of the children?

"Village School"

"Children's Puppet Theatre"

Capturing Children's Emotions

Looking at children in different settings, you can see the honesty of their expressions. They may be happy or sad, playful, or and serious, but there is always integrity about their emotions. Here are two photographs of children. One is called "Village School" by Margaret Bourke-White, who included this picture in her book *Eyes on Russia,* published in 1934. The other is called "Children's Puppet Theatre, Paris 1963" by Alfred Eisenstadt. In both photographs, the children are staring at something, but the moods of the two are completely different.

In the Bourke-White photograph, you see rows of children in a confined, dark room. The only light that is shining is on the faces of the boys. In fact, they seem to be simply heads not bodies. Their hair is short, which makes their ears very noticeable. A few upper torsos are visible, some of them in light shirts and others in dark colors. The photographer's point of view emphasizes the boys' heads, giving a serious mood to the photograph. The boys are sitting up straight with their arms out of view. They are in four rows with all the faces staring straight ahead. Arranged in an inverted triangle, they look a little like bowling pins ready for someone to knock down. However, there are large gaps between them. None of the boys is touching the other, and there appears to be no communication. This arrangement creates a feeling of isolation. The periphery is dark, and we do not see the object or person the boys are looking at. The wooden benches they are sitting on look uncomfortable.

The children in the Eisenstadt photograph, both boys and girls, are all bunched together. We see mostly their heads, but sometimes only parts of faces are visible. There are five prominent faces in the foreground that you can see completely. In the background the faces are cut off, and sometimes you only see the tops of the children's heads. The children are touching. In fact, in the lower right corner, one little girl is resting her head on another slightly taller girl. The main center of interest is a little boy whose mouth is wide open and whose right hand is shooting out in front of him. The expressions on the faces of the children vary greatly. Some are laughing out loud while others are holding their hands over their faces. A few are screaming and some are in awe. One boy is covering his ears, which might mean the sound is too loud for him.

In "Village School," the light is shining only on the children's heads. This suggests that their intellect is being emphasized while their emotions have to be covered up. And yet even though there is something a little frightening about this photograph, all the boys have dignity and appear to have strong individual personalities. The boy in front, whose face is the largest and whose body you cannot see at all, has a look of hope. Even though the school may be strict, the children are not defeated. In "Children's Puppet Theatre, Paris 1963," the feeling is loud and bright and fun. The children are able to release their emotions and show exactly how they feel. There is no inhibition. These children are outdoors having a good time. The periphery is light with many shadings of gray. Although there is no color, the textures of the gray woolen sweaters give the photograph life. Unlike the schoolboys, these children are not in neat rows but seem to be in motion, touching, leaning, and hugging. They also have strong personalities, which are openly displayed, not quietly revealed as in the "Village School."

Two groups of children are depicted in these two photographs. In one we feel the strength and stillness of the boys. One is structured and the other is free. One shows contrast by using light and dark. It focuses on the children's faces. The other also focuses on the children's faces, but does so by capturing many extreme and diverse expressions. The two photographs show movement versus stillness. And yet in both we are drawn in by the personalities of the children and their great individuality.

Analyzing the student essay

A. Respond to the student essay by answering the questions below in full sentences.

1. How does Margaret Bourke-White convey a sense of isolation in her photograph? _____

   _____

   _____

2. What is the difference in how the children are positioned in the two photographs? _____

   _____

   _____

3. What is the mood in Eisenstadt's photograph? What evidence is there to illustrate this mood? _____

   _____

   _____

4. Why are the expressions on the children's faces in both photographs so important? _____

   _____

   _____

5. What are the positive elements in the "Village School"? _____

   _____

   _____

B. Examine the organization of the student essay by answering the questions below. Then compare your answers with a partner.

1. Circle the hook.

2. Write the background information of the introduction on the lines below.

   _____

   _____

3. Underline the thesis statement.

4. Write down the main message of body paragraph 1 in your own words.

   _____

   _____

5. What elements are described in body paragraph 2?

    _____ a. main center of interest   _____ e. mood

    _____ b. background   _____ f. viewpoint

    _____ c. foreground   _____ g. contrast

    _____ d. periphery

6. What elements are compared in body paragraph 3? _____

_____

_____

7. What similarities and differences are restated in the conclusion? _____

_____

_____

Exercise 5   ## Writing an Outline

Review your brainstorming ideas and your freewriting exercise. Then use the chart below to write an outline for a reaction essay about the two photographs on page 146.

Introduction

Hook: _____

_____

_____

Background information: _____

_____

_____

Thesis statement: _____

_____

_____

"playing in street sprinkler"

Body Paragraph 1

Topic sentence: _____

_____

_____

Analysis: _____

_____

_____

Supporting evidence: _____

_____

_____

Body Paragraph 1

"children playing baseball"

Topic sentence: _____

_____

Analysis: _____

_____

Supporting evidence: _____

_____

_____

Body Paragraph 3

comparison of both photographs

Topic sentence: _____

_____

Comparison and contrast of the effect of the photograph on the viewer: _____

_____

_____

Conclusion

Restatement of similarities and differences: _____

_____

_____

Conclusions about effect of photographs on the viewer: _____

_____

_____

In Part 3 you will . . .

- learn about prepositional phrases.
- learn about similes.
- write a first draft of your reaction essay.

PART 3

Developing Your Ideas

Exercise 1   **Reading a student essay**

Read the essay about the photographs on page 152. How does this writer respond to the children's faces?

The Expressions of Youth

Seeing the emotions expressed in children's faces can elicit powerful responses from the viewer. Children laughing hysterically, teeth showing, can brighten up your day. Thoughtful, solemn, or introverted feelings can touch you deeply. The photographs, Margaret Bourke-White's "Village School" and Alfred Eisenstadt's "Children's Puppet Theater, Paris 1963" both have children as the central figures. "Village School" shows the more serious side, while "Children's Puppet Theater" reveals the freedom of youth. Although different, both photographs display a transparency of feeling reflected in the body language and facial expressions of the subjects.

In "Children's Puppet Theater," a crowd of excited and surprised children are all gathered together looking at the puppet theater. Some of them are screaming and others look astonished. They are reacting to something funny. In the center, one child has his arms raised pointing toward the stage, which we cannot see. Others are covering their mouths and cheeks, and one boy is covering his ears. Perhaps he does not like what he hears. Some are holding on to each other as if they are shocked. What makes this picture so special is that the children are not posed, but have been caught in a vivid moment of spontaneous joy. Their expressions are so real that we can almost imagine the puppets they are watching. In the background, the light is diffuse, which suggests endless rows of children.

The group of boys in the "Village School" are all seated, one behind the other, in a closed space on benches that look like church pews. On the periphery, the room looks barren, with nothing to brighten it up. The picture is dark. The boys are passive without any signs of emotion on their faces, and most of them are wearing somber clothing. This contrasts sharply with the light that shines only on their faces and heads. The center of focus is the boy in the foreground. He is completely alone in his row, isolated from his peers. It seems as if the children are oppressed and fearful. Perhaps the person who is in charge is very strict and severe, and as a consequence the children behave well and remain quiet and calm.

Both photographs depict children of about the same age, who are looking at someone or something that the viewer cannot see. The "Village School" is made up of only boys while the other includes both boys and girls. Having only boys gives the impression that the atmosphere is more rigid, and this is emphasized by the way the boys are positioned. "Children's Puppet Theater, Paris 1963" features many tones and shades of grey to white and many different textures in the clothing. This photograph has a lightness about it in contrast to the intense gloomy quality of the other.

Photographs have an amazing power to transmit energy to the viewer. Diverse emotions that emerge from the images, such as fear, happiness, anxiety, and hope, can be experienced in an instant. These photos captivate the viewer not by what the children are watching but by how they react. We are drawn into their reality.

Exercise 2   Analyzing the student essay

A. Respond to the essay above by answering the questions below in full sentences.

1. How are the children's emotions communicated in both "Village School" and "Children's Puppet Theater, Paris 1963"? _____

   _____

   _____

2. What images in "Village School" create a somber mood? _____

_____

_____

3. What impression does a photograph with only boys produce? _____

_____

_____

4. Who does the writer suggest the children are fearful of in "Village School?"

_____

_____

B. Examine the organization of the essay by answering the questions below. Then compare your answers with a partner.

1. Circle the hook.

2. Underline the thesis statement. Rewrite it in your own words. _____

_____

_____

3. What details does the writer provide in body paragraph 1 to describe the mood of spontaneity in the photograph? _____

_____

_____

4. Give an example of contrast in body paragraph 2. _____

_____

_____

5. What elements are compared in body paragraph 3? _____

_____

_____

6. What conclusion does the writer draw about the effect of the photographs?

_____

_____

Language Focus

Prepositions and Prepositional Phrases

Prepositions are words such as *at, in, on,* and *next to.* A preposition can be used in a phrase with a noun or pronoun to show relationships between people and objects—this is called a prepositional phrase. Prepositional phrases can also be used to show location and special order.

The children are sitting **on** <u>wooden benches</u>.

Prepositional Phrases Showing Spatial Relationships

Prepositions like *by, for, of, to, with,* and *on* can be used in prepositional phrases to show spatial relationships between people and objects.

Three girls are throwing bread crumbs **to** <u>the birds</u>.

Prepositions Showing Location and Spatial Order

Prepositional phrases can also be used in descriptions to show location and spatial order.

People are standing **in front of** <u>the building</u>.

Here are a few common prepositions and prepositional phrases that can be used to show location and spatial order.

in front of	behind	in the foreground	in the background
above	over	below	beneath
in the center	on the left	on the right	on the periphery
on the sides	next to		

Exercise 3 **Identifying prepositions**

Choose the correct preposition from the box to complete the following sentences.

by for of to in ~~on~~

1. The little girl is resting her head _____on_____ her mother's shoulder.

2. The three children are posing _____ the camera

3. The two women were having lunch _____ the pool.

4. On the left side _____ the photograph are two large trees.

5. The woman _____ the flowered hat is sitting in the front row.

6. The little boy was waving goodbye _____ his grandmother.

Using prepositional phrases in sentences

Look at the photograph "Children Playing Baseball" on page 146. Write a sentence about each of the items below. Use a prepositional phrase from the Language Focus on page 161 in each sentence.

1. a young boy

   _____

2. rows of laundry

   _____

3. a group of children

   _____

4. a barrel

   _____

5. several tall buildings

   _____

6. a sidewalk

   _____

Language Focus

Similes

A simile is the comparison of two unlike things. Similes create images that enrich a piece of writing; they can also communicate meaning in an indirect or surprising way. They are often used in literature and poetry.

He cried **like a baby.**

In the example above, the writer uses the simile *like a baby* to describe a crying person. Babies are helpless, and by comparing the man to a baby, the writer communicates a sense of helplessness.

Simile Structure

• A simile can use the preposition *like* + a noun or a noun phrase.

The rollers in the girl's hair look **like** <u>a peacock's feathers</u>.

• A simile can use *as . . . as* + a noun or a noun phrase. This kind of simile also uses an adjective.

In the newspaper photograph, he looked **as** <u>proud</u> **as** <u>an eagle</u>.

Exercise 5   Using Similes

A. Match the first half of each sentence with the second half.

_C_ 1. They are seated on   a. like a jaguar.
         benches that look

_____ 2. Her smile is   b. as playful as a young puppy.

_____ 3. He runs   c. like church pews.

_____ 4. The child is   d. like thick velvet curtains.

_____ 5. The street is   e. as bright as a summer day.

_____ 6. The shadows are   f. as colorful as an amusement park.

B. Choose similes from part A and think about what each simile suggests. Then write sentences that explain what these similes mean.

1. <u>The church pews suggest that the boys are in church and are</u>
   <u>therefore sitting quietly and respectfully.</u>
   _____

2. _____
   _____
   _____

3. _____
   _____
   _____

4. _____
   _____
   _____

Exercise 6   Writing a first draft

Review your outline. Then write your first draft of a five-paragraph reaction essay in response to the two photographs on page 152.

Exercise 7   Peer editing a first draft

After you write your first draft, exchange it with a partner. Answer the questions on the checklist on page 164. Write comments or questions for your partner. Then read your partner's comments about your first draft and revise it as necessary.

Editor's Checklist

Put a check (✓) as appropriate. Write answers in complete sentences in the lines provided.

☐ 1. Does the introduction include an interesting hook? If so, write it here.

    _____

    _____

☐ 2. Does the introduction include the titles of the photographs and the names of the photographers?

☐ 3. Did the writer use any of the photographic terms below? If yes, circle the ones used:

    a. main center of interest   e. mood

    b. background   f. viewpoint

    c. foreground   g. contrast

    d. periphery

☐ 4. Did the writer analyze the message of each photograph?

☐ 5. Does paragraph 4 explain the similarities and differences between the two photographs?

☐ 6. Circle any similes the writer used and comment below on their effectiveness.

    _____

    _____

☐ 7. Does the conclusion evaluate the effects of the photographs? Restate the effects below.

    _____

    _____

In Part 4 you will . . .

- learn about restrictive and nonrestrictive relative clauses.
- edit your first draft for grammatical mistakes.

PART 4

Editing Your Writing

Now that you have written your first draft, it is time to edit. Editing involves making changes to your writing to improve it and correct mistakes.

Language Focus

Relative Clauses

Relative clauses (also called adjective clauses) modify nouns or noun phrases. They are dependent clauses and must be attached to a main clause.

- A relative clause must always follow the noun to which it refers.

- There are two types of relative clauses: restrictive and nonrestrictive.

Restrictive Relative Clauses

A restrictive relative clause gives essential information that helps identify or define the noun or noun phrase it modifies.

That is the <u>woman</u> **who sits next to me in French class.**

- In restrictive clauses use the relative pronouns <u>who</u> or <u>that</u> for people, and <u>which</u> or <u>that</u> for things and animals.

- Do not use a comma between the noun and the relative pronoun.

Nonrestrictive Relative Clauses

A nonrestrictive relative clause gives extra information about a noun or noun phrase.

<u>Walker Evans,</u> **who collaborated with the writer James Agee,** was a famous 20th century photographer.

- In nonrestrictive relative clauses, use *who* for people and *which* for things.

- Use commas to separate the clause from the rest of the sentence.

⚠ Do not use *that* in a nonrestrictive relative clause.

Restrictive Relative Clauses After the Main Clause

MAIN CLAUSE		RELATIVE CLAUSE		
	NOUN	SUBJECT RELATIVE PRONOUN	VERB	
I know	a photographer	**who** **that**	**travels**	all over the world.
They take	photographs	**which** **that**	**appear**	in museums.

Restrictive Relative Clauses Inside the Main Clause

MAIN CLAUSE				
	RELATIVE CLAUSE			
NOUN	SUBJECT RELATIVE PRONOUN	VERB		
The photographer	**who** **that**	**travels**	**all over the world**	won't use a digital camera.
The photographs	**which** **that**	**appear**	**in museums**	are extremely famous.

Nonrestrictive Relative Clauses After the Main Clause

MAIN CLAUSE		RELATIVE CLAUSE		
	NOUN	SUBJECT RELATIVE PRONOUN	VERB	
I know	Sam,	**who**	**travels**	all over the world.
Everyone likes	the photographs,	**which**	**are**	extremely expensive.

Nonrestrictive Relative Clauses Inside the Main Clause

MAIN CLAUSE	RELATIVE CLAUSE			
NOUN	SUBJECT RELATIVE PRONOUN	VERB		
Sam,	**who**	**travels**	**all over the world,**	won't use a digital camera.
The photographs,	**which**	**are**	**extremely expensive,**	appear in museums.

Exercise 1 Identifying restrictive and nonrestrictive clauses

Underline the relative clauses. If the sentence is a restrictive relative clause, write _R_. If the sentence is a nonrestrictive clause, write _NR_.

_R_ 1. The photographer <u>who was also a set designer</u> was Cecil Beaton.

____ 2. Mathew Brady, who was one of the first photojournalists, took pictures of the U.S. Civil War.

____ 3. The photographs that were taken by Lewis Hines depict children working in factories.

____ 4. Many of the people that were photographed by Ben Shahn during the 1930s were tenant farmers.

Combining sentences using restrictive relative clauses

Use a restrictive relative clause to combine each pair of sentences.

1. Photographs require special lighting. They are taken indoors.

   <u>Photographs that are taken indoors require special lighting.</u>

2. Subjects should not face the sun. They are being photographed outdoors.

   _____

   _____

3. Ansel Adams took photographs. They show magnificent scenes in nature.

   _____

   _____

4. Film should not be used. It has expired.

   _____

   _____

Combining sentences using nonrestrictive relative clauses

Use a nonrestrictive relative clause to combine each pair of sentences.

1. Photojournalism focuses on newsworthy events. It is one career path for photographers.

   <u>Photojournalism, which is one career path for photographers, focuses</u>
   <u>on newsworthy events.</u>

2. Thomas Edison invented the light bulb. He contributed to the film industry.

   _____

   _____

3. The digital camera is used worldwide. It allows people to send photos over the Internet.

   _____

   _____

4. Louis Daguerre was a French inventor. He developed the diorama.

   _____

   _____

Language Focus

Relative Clauses with *Whose*

Whose is the relative pronoun that shows possession. It takes the place of the pronouns *his, her, its, their* or the possessive form of the noun. It is always followed by a noun.

- *Whose* is used for both people and things.

- *Whose* can be used with both restrictive and nonrestrictive clauses.
  The girl **whose hair is in rollers** is getting her hair straightened.
  Maria, **whose father owns that factory,** is one of our clients.

Exercise 4   **Combining sentences with whose**

Use a restrictive or nonrestrictive relative clause with *whose* to combine each pair of sentences.

1. The boy is standing by the tree. His overalls are torn.
   The boy whose overalls are torn is standing by the tree.
   _____

2. There are many photographs. Their sizes have been changed.
   _____
   _____

3. Richard Avedon was a world-renowned portrait photographer. His pictures were of famous celebrities.
   _____
   _____

4. Yousuf Karsh was born in Armenia. His photograph of Winston Churchill brought him international fame.
   _____
   _____

5. Galleries attract large crowds. Their exhibits are very controversial.
   _____
   _____

Exercise 5   Editing a paragraph

Read the paragraph. Correct the mistakes. There are seven mistakes, including two punctuation mistakes.

The camera, was invented in 1837, has had many different professional and personal uses. One of the earliest professional photographers was Julia Cameron, who objective was to make photographs the way a painter would create a painting. These photographs looked like the portraits, that were painted then. Mathew Brady, who was the greatest photojournalist of the Civil War period informed the public about the realities of war. Photojournalism was also used to depict life during the Great Depression. For example, photographers like Dorothea Lange took emotional photos of the dust storms in Oklahoma, whose displaced families from their homes. Photos have become a necessity for families they want to chronicle the milestones in their childrens' lives. Photos, are an essential part of any wedding, are cherished by brides all over the world.

Exercise 6   Editing your first draft and rewriting

Review your essay for language mistakes. Use the checklist below. Then write a final draft.

Editor's Checklist

Put a check (✓) as appropriate.

☐ 1. Did you use restrictive relative clauses with *who* or *that?*

☐ 2. Did you use restrictive relative clauses for things with *that* or *which?*

☐ 3. Did you use non-restrictive relative clauses for people? If yes, did you add commas?

☐ 4. Did you use non-restrictive relative clauses with things? If yes did you use *which?*

☐ 5. Did you use *whose* for possession with people and things? If yes, is *whose* followed by a noun or noun phrase?

In Part 5 you will . . .

- review the elements of reaction writing.
- practice writing under a time limit.

Putting It All Together

In this part of the unit, you will complete six exercises to improve your accuracy, write a timed essay to improve your fluency, and explore topics for further writing.

Exercise 1 | Identifying prepositions

Choose the correct preposition from the box to complete the following sentences.

by	for	of	in	with	on

1. Three tired children are reclining ＿＿＿＿＿＿ the bed.

2. The smiling newspaper boy is standing ＿＿＿＿＿＿ the fence.

3. The filmmakers organized a benefit ＿＿＿＿＿＿ the disabled.

4. The man ＿＿＿＿＿＿ the pipe is sitting next to his wife.

5. The street musicians were playing in front ＿＿＿＿＿＿ the subway station.

6. The woman ＿＿＿＿＿＿ the pink dress looks sad.

Exercise 2 | Using similes

Match the first half of each sentence with the second half.

＿＿＿ 1. The laughter of children is   a. as strong as an ox.

＿＿＿ 2. The ballerina is   b. like a native.

＿＿＿ 3. The professor speaks Spanish   c. like a pro.

＿＿＿ 4. The football player is   d. like a ray of hope.

＿＿＿ 5. He plays baseball   e. as delicate as a cherry blossom.

Exercise 3 | Combining sentences using restrictive relative clauses

Use a restrictive relative clause to combine each pair of sentences.

1. The cinematographer is George Lucas. He is best known for special effects.

＿＿＿＿＿＿＿＿＿＿＿＿＿＿＿＿＿＿＿＿＿＿＿＿＿＿＿＿＿＿＿＿＿＿＿＿＿

＿＿＿＿＿＿＿＿＿＿＿＿＿＿＿＿＿＿＿＿＿＿＿＿＿＿＿＿＿＿＿＿＿＿＿＿＿

2. The photos were overexposed. We took the photos on the beach.

＿＿＿＿＿＿＿＿＿＿＿＿＿＿＿＿＿＿＿＿＿＿＿＿＿＿＿＿＿＿＿＿＿＿＿＿＿

＿＿＿＿＿＿＿＿＿＿＿＿＿＿＿＿＿＿＿＿＿＿＿＿＿＿＿＿＿＿＿＿＿＿＿＿＿

3. I broke my camera lens. It was for my new camera.

_____

_____

4. The camera case was stolen. It was bought in Italy.

_____

_____

5. The Eiffel Tower was crowded with people. They were all taking pictures at the same time.

_____

_____

6. Reporters invade people's privacy. They take pictures of celebrities.

_____

_____

Exercise 4   **Combining sentences using nonrestrictive relative clauses**

Use a nonrestrictive relative clause to combine each pair of sentences.

1. Nobuoshi Araki was born in Tokyo. He is one of the most famous modern Japanese photographers.

_____

_____

2. The camera obscura was a type of primitive camera. It was made from a box with a small pinhole opening.

_____

_____

3. Alfred Stieglitz worked hard to make people accept photography as an art form. He was married to the famous painter Georgia O'Keefe.

_____

_____

4. The Polaroid camera produced instant photographs. It was invented by Edwin Land in 1948.

_____

_____

5. The first practical process of photography was invented by Daguerre. He was born in 1789.

_____

_____

6. The first Kodak Brownie camera was mass produced in 1900. It cost $1.00.

_____

_____

Exercise 5 **Combining sentences with whose**

Use a restrictive or nonrestrictive relative clause *whose* to combine each pair of sentences.

1. The man filed a police report. His camera was stolen.

_____

_____

2. The woman lives in New York. Her bag was lost.

_____

_____

3. The local 24-hour photo shop has a booming business. Its promotional advertisements entice lots of customers.

_____

_____

4. The $500 prize went to the young photographer. Her subject matter was her cat.

_____

_____

5. The students were advised to reapply in the spring. Their applications were turned down.

_____

_____

Exercise 6 **Editing a paragraph**

Read the paragraph and edit as necessary. There are six mistakes.

For anyone thinking of photography as a career, there are many exciting alternatives. For those who ambition is to be where the action is and who are not afraid of taking risks, photojournalism provides many thrilling possibilities. However, you may find yourself in a forest fire that could be life-threatening. Do you like to work in the outdoors? Then wildlife photography is a job who captures animals in their natural habitat. If creating posters, magazine layouts, and brochures in a large corporation sounds interesting to you, there's advertising photography. Law-enforcement photographers shoot crime scenes, who help police solve important cases. Sports photographers, their job is to freeze one perfect moment in time, often need to take one or two rolls of film with quick succession to get the desired shot. Fashion photography, who may seem glamorous to some people, is really focused on selling clothing and can be very competitive. Do you ever wonder how restaurant menus can make the French fries look better in the picture than on your plate? Then you might want to take pictures for food. However, taking pictures is not as easy as like baking bread. Taking a photograph is like painting a picture. It requires skill, creativity, and an eye for detail.

TIMED WRITING: 60 minutes

Write a five-paragraph reaction essay in response to these two photographs. Before you begin to write, review the suggested time management strategy below.

BRAINSTORMING: 5 minutes

Write down ideas and vocabulary for your brainstorm on a separate piece of paper. You may want to use a chart similar to the one on page 150.

OUTLINING: 5 minutes

Write an outline for your essay in the form below.

Introduction

Hook: _____

_____

_____

Background information: _____

_____

_____

Thesis statement: _____

_____

_____

photograph 1

Body Paragraph 1

Topic sentence: _____

_____

_____

Analysis: _____

_____

_____

Supporting evidence: _____

_____

_____

photograph 2

Body Paragraph 2

Topic sentence: _____

_____

_____

Analysis: _____

_____

_____

Supporting evidence: _____

_____

_____

comparison of photographs

Body Paragraph 3

Topic sentence: _____

_____

_____

Comparison and contrast of the effect of the photograph on the viewer: _____

_____

_____

Conclusion

Restatement of similarities and differences: _____

_____

_____

Conclusions about effect of photographs on the viewer: _____

_____

_____

Step 3 **WRITING: 40 minutes**

Use your brainstorming notes and outline to write your essay on a separate piece of paper.

Step 4 **EDITING: 10 minutes**

When you have finished your first draft, check it for mistakes, using the checklist below.

Editor's Checklist

Put a check (✓) as appropriate.

☐ 1. Does the introduction provide background information?

☐ 2. Did you include an analysis of each photograph in body paragraphs 2 and 3?

☐ 3. Did you explain the similarities and differences between the photographs in paragraph 4?

☐ 4. Did you use restrictive relative clauses?

☐ 5. Did you use nonrestrictive relative clauses?

☐ 6. Did you use *whose* to show possession in restrictive or nonrestrictive clauses? If yes, is *whose* followed by a noun?

☐ 7. Did you use any prepositional phrases?

☐ 8. Did you use any similes?

Write a five-paragraph reaction essay on one of the following topics.

- Two photographs by the same photographer on the Internet or in a local gallery. Here are the names of some photographers:

    Cartier-Bresson

    Ben Shahn

    Helen Levitt

    Manuel Bravo

    Walker Evans

    Ansel Adams

- Two family photographs taken at different time periods.
- Two examples of photojournalism from a magazine, newspaper, or book.
- Two photos of products used in advertisements. Explain why their messages are strong or not.
- Your own photographs of the same subject, but in different settings. For example, if you choose parks, take pictures of two different parks. Here are some other themes:

    an owner and her pet

    a mother and child

    a sport event

    street vendors

    school playgrounds

    billboards

Appendices

Appendix I: **Advanced Punctuation Issues**

Punctuation with Main Clauses

A main clause that stands alone is a sentence and is followed by a period.

- William Shakespeare was an Elizabethan playwright.

Two main clauses can be connected to form a compound sentence by using one of the coordinating conjunctions *and, but, yet, so, or* or *for*. Use a comma (,) before the coordinating conjunction.

- William Shakespeare was an important playwright, **but** he also wrote very fine short sonnets.

Two main clauses that are very close in meaning can be connected by a semicolon (;).

- Shakespeare's Romeo and Juliet is one of his most popular tragedies; it is performed throughout the world.

Punctuation with Transitional Expressions

Transitional expressions begin a sentence and are separated from the main clause by a comma. Common expressions include *for example, moreover, however, therefore, first, next,* and *in fact*.

- I enjoy writing in my journal. **However,** I don't like writing letters.

When transitional expressions join two sentences, they are preceded by a semicolon and followed by a comma.

- I enjoy writing in my journal; **however,** I don't like writing letters.

Punctuation with Main and Dependent Clauses

Some subordinating conjunctions that introduce dependent clauses and include *because, when, before, although* and *since*.
When the dependent clause begins a sentence, place a comma after it.

- When I read my speech at graduation, all my friends and family were amazed.

When the dependent clause comes at the end of the sentence, omit the comma.

- All my friends and family were amazed when I read my speech at graduation.

Punctuation with Conditional Sentences

When the *if* clause begins the sentence, use a comma.

- **If** I get a new job, I will make more money.

When the *if* clause follows the main clause, do not use a comma.

- I will make more money **if** I get the new job.

Punctuation with Relative Clauses

In restrictive clauses use the relative pronouns *who* or *that* for people, *which* or *that* for things and animals, and *whose* to show ownership or belonging. Do not use a comma between the noun and the relative pronoun.

- The song **that** won first prize was by a famous hip-hop artist.
- The hip-hop artist **who** won the award studied at my music school.

In nonrestrictive relative clauses, use *who* for people and *which* for things. Use commas to separate the clause from the rest of the sentence.

- Walker Evans, **who** collaborated with the writer James Agee, was a famous 20th century photographer.
- The Mona Lisa, **which** was painted by Leonardo Da Vinci, hangs in the Louvre.

Connectors with Noun Phrases

The connectors *because of, due to,* and *as a result of* introduce a noun phrase. When the noun phrase comes at the beginning of a sentence, it is followed by a comma. When it comes at the end of a sentence, no comma is used.

- **Due to** the heavy traffic, we were late for class.
- We were late for class **due to** the heavy traffic.

Appendix II: **Gerunds and Infinitives**

Gerunds
Verb + Gerund

acknowledge	deny	involve	recall
admit	discuss	keep	recommend
appreciate	dislike	mean	regret
avoid	enjoy	mention	report
celebrate	feel like	mind	resume
consider	finish	miss	suggest
delay	go	practice	understand

Verb with Preposition + Gerund

adapt to	argue about	care about	depend on
adjust to	ask about	complain about	disapprove of
agree on	believe in	consist of	forgive for
apologize for	blame for	decide on	help with

Be + Adjective + Preposition + Gerund

be afraid of	be glad about	be known for	be successful in
be angry about	be happy about	be nervous about	be tired of
be concerned with	be interested in	be proud of	be upset about
be familiar with	be jealous of	be sad about	be used for

Infinitives
Verb + Infinitive

agree	decide	intend	resolve
appear	decline	manage	seem
arrange	demand	plan	struggle
care	fail	pretend	volunteer
claim	hope	refuse	wait

Verb + Object + Infinitive

advise	get	persuade	tell
command	hire	remind	trust
convince	invite	require	urge
force	order	teach	warn

Verb + (Object) + Infinitive

ask	desire	need	promise
beg	expect	offer	want
choose	help	pay	wish
dare	know	prepare	would like

Appendix III: **Glossary**

Adapted from the **Grammar Sense** *Glossary of Grammar Terms*

action verb A verb that describes a thing that someone or something does. An action verb does not describe a state or condition.

> Sam **rang** the bell.
> It **rains** a lot here.

active sentence In active sentences, the agent (the noun that is performing the action) is in subject position and the receiver (the noun that receives or is a result of the action) is in object position. In the following sentence, the subject **Alex** performed the action, and the object **letter** received the action.

> Alex mailed the letter.

adjective A word that describes or modifies the meaning of a noun.

> the **orange** car   a **strange** noise

adverb A word that describes or modifies the meaning of a verb, another adverb, an adjective, or a sentence. Many adverbs answer such questions as *How? When? Where?* or *How often?* They often end in **-ly.**

> She ran **quickly**.   She ran **very** quickly.
> a **really** hot day   **Maybe** she'll leave.

adverbial phrase A phrase that functions as an adverb.

> Amy spoke **very softly**.

affirmative statement A sentence that does not have a negative verb.

> Linda went to the movies.

agreement The subject and verb of a clause must agree in number. If the subject is singular, the verb form is also singular. If the subject is plural, the verb form is also plural.

> **He comes** home early.   **They come** home early.

article The words **a, an,** and **the** in English. Articles are used to introduce and identify nouns.

> **a** potato   **an** onion   **the** supermarket

auxiliary verb A verb that is used before main verbs (or other auxiliary verbs) in a sentence. Auxiliary verbs are usually used in questions and negative sentences. **Do, have,** and **be** can act as auxiliary verbs. Modals (**may, can, will,** and so on) are also auxiliary verbs.

> **Do** you have the time?   The car **was** speeding.
> I **have** never been to Italy.   I **may** be late.

base form The form of a verb without any verb endings; the infinitive form without *to*.

> sleep   be   stop

clause A group of words that has a subject and a verb. *See also* **dependent clause** and **main clause.**

> If I leave, ... when he speaks.
> The rain stopped.   . . . that I saw.

common noun A noun that refers to any of a class of people, animals, places, things, or ideas. Common nouns are not capitalized.

> man   cat   city   pencil   grammar

comparative A form of an adjective, adverb, or noun that is used to express differences between two items or situations.

> This book is **heavier than** that one.
> He runs **more quickly than** his brother.
> A CD costs **more money than** a cassette.

complex sentence A sentence that has a main clause and one or more dependent clauses.

> When the bell rang, we were finishing dinner.

compound sentence A sentence that has two main clauses separated by a comma and a conjunction, or by a semi-colon.

> She is very talented; she can sing and dance.

conditional sentence A sentence that expresses a real or unreal situation in the *if* clause, and the (real or unreal) expected result in the main clause.

> If I have time, I will travel to Africa.
> If I had time, I would travel to Africa.

countable noun A common noun that can be counted. It usually has both a singular and a plural form.

> orange — oranges   woman — women

definite article The word **the** in English. It is used to identify nouns based on assumptions about what information the speaker and listener share about the noun. The definite article is also used for making general statements about a whole class or group of nouns.

> Please give me **the** key.
> **The** scorpion is dangerous.

dependent clause A clause that cannot stand alone as a sentence because it depends on the main clause to complete the meaning of the sentence. Also called *subordinate clause.*

> I'm going home **after he calls**.

determiner A word such as **a, an, the, this, that, these, those, my, some, a few,** and **three** that is used before a noun to limit its meaning in some way.

> **those** videos

future A time that is to come. The future is expressed in English with **will, be going to,** the simple present, or the present continuous. These different forms of the future often have different meanings and uses.

> I **will** help you later.
> David **is going to** call later.
> The train **leaves** at 6:05 this evening.
> I**'m driving** to Toronto tomorrow.

gerund An **-ing** form of a verb that is used in place of a noun or pronoun to name an activity or a state.

> **Skiing** is fun.   He doesn't like **being sick**.

if **clause** A dependent clause that begins with **if** and expresses a real or unreal situation.

> **If I have the time,** I'll paint the kitchen.
> **If I had the time,** I'd paint the kitchen.

indefinite article The words **a** and **an** in English. Indefinite articles introduce a noun as a member of a class of nouns or make generalizations about a whole class or group of nouns.

> **An** ocean is **a** large body of water.

independent clause *See* **main clause**.

indirect object A noun or pronoun used after some verbs that refers to the person who receives the direct object of a sentence.

> John wrote a letter to **Mary**.
> Please buy some milk for **us**.

infinitive A verb form that includes **to** + the base form of a verb. An infinitive is used in place of a noun or pronoun to name an activity or situation expressed by a verb.

> Do you like **to swim**?

intransitive verb A verb that cannot be followed by an object.

> We finally **arrived**.

main clause A clause that can be used by itself as a sentence. Also called *independent clause*.

> I'm going home.

main verb A verb that can be used alone in a sentence. A main verb can also occur with an auxiliary verb.

> I **ate** lunch at 11:30.
> Kate can't **eat** lunch today.

modal The auxiliary verbs **can, could, may, might, must, should, will,** and **would**. They modify the meaning of a main verb by expressing ability, authority, formality, politeness, or various degrees of certainty. Also called *modal auxiliary*.

> You **should** take something for your headache.
> Applicants **must** have a high school diploma.

negative statement A sentence with a negative verb.

> I **didn't see** that movie.

noun A word that typically refers to a person, animal, place, thing, or idea.

> Tom   rabbit   store   computer   mathematics

noun clause A dependent clause that can occur in the same place as a noun, pronoun, or noun phrase in a sentence. Noun clauses begin with **wh-** words, **if, whether,** or **that**.

> I don't know **where he is**.
> I wonder **if he's coming**.
> I don't know **whether it's true**.
> I think **that it's a lie**.

noun phrase A phrase formed by a noun and its modifiers. A noun phrase can substitute for a noun in a sentence.

> She drank **milk**.
> She drank **chocolate milk**.
> She drank **the milk**.

object A noun, pronoun, or noun phrase that follows a transitive verb or a preposition.

> He likes **pizza**.   Go with **her**.
> She likes **him**.   Steve threw **the ball**.

passive sentence Passive sentences emphasize the receiver of an action by changing the usual order of the subject and object in a sentence. In the sentence below, the subject **(The letter)** does not perform the action; it receives the action or is the result of an action. The passive is formed with a form of **be** + the past participle of a transitive verb.

> The letter was mailed yesterday.

past continuous A verb form that expresses an action or situation in progress at a specific time in the past. The past continuous is formed with **was** or **were** + verb + **-ing**. Also called *past progressive*.

> A: What **were** you **doing** last night at eight o'clock?
> B: I **was studying**.

past participle A past verb form that may differ from the simple past form of some irregular verbs. It is used to form the present perfect, for example.

> I have never **seen** that movie.

phrasal verb A two- or three-word verb such as **turn down** or **run out of**. The meaning of a phrasal verb is usually different from the meanings of its individual words.

> She **turned down** the job offer.
> Don't **run out of** gas on the freeway.

phrase A group of words that can form a grammatical unit. A phrase can take the form of a noun phrase, verb phrase, adjective phrase, adverbial phrase, or prepositional phrase. This means it can act as a noun, verb, adjective, adverb, or preposition.

> The **tall man** left.   She spoke **too fast**.
> Lee **hit the ball**.   They ran **down the stairs**.

preposition A word such as **at, in, on,** or **to,** that links nouns, pronouns, and gerunds to other words.

prepositional phrase A phrase that consists of a preposition followed by a noun or noun phrase.

> on Sunday   under the table

present continuous A verb form that indicates that an activity is in progress, temporary, or changing. It is formed with **be** + verb + **-ing.** Also called *present progressive.*

> I'm **watering** the garden.
> Ruth **is working** for her uncle.

present perfect A verb form that expresses a connection between the past and the present. It indicates indefinite past time, recent past time, or continuing past time. The present perfect is formed with **have** + the past participle of the main verb.

> I**'ve seen** that movie.
> The manager **has** just **resigned**.
> We**'ve been** here for three hours.

pronoun A word that can replace a noun or noun phrase. **I, you, he, she, it, mine,** and **yours** are some examples of pronouns.

quantity expression A word or words that occur before a noun to express a quantity or amount of that noun.

> **a lot of** rain   **few** books   **four** trucks

simple past A verb form that expresses actions and situations that were completed at a definite time in the past.

> Carol **ate** lunch.   She **was** hungry.

simple present A verb form that expresses general statements, especially about habitual or repeated activities and permanent situations.

> Every morning I **catch** the 8:00 bus.
> The earth **is** round.

stative verb A type of verb that is not usually used in the continuous form because it expresses a condition or state that is not changing. **Know, love, see,** and **smell** are some examples.

subject A noun, pronoun, or noun phrase that precedes the verb phrase in a sentence. The subject is closely related to the verb as the doer or experiencer of the action or state, or closely related to the noun that is being described in a sentence with *be.*

> **Erica** kicked the ball.
> **The park** is huge.

subordinate clause *See* **dependent clause.**

superlative A form of an adjective, adverb, or noun that is used to rank an item or situation first or last in a group of three or more.

> This perfume has **the strongest** scent.
> He speaks **the fastest** of all.
> That machine makes **the most noise** of the three.

tense The form of a verb that shows past, present, and future time.

> He **lives** in New York now.
> He **lived** in Washington two years ago.
> He**'ll live** in Toronto next year.

time clause A dependent clause that begins with a word such as **while, when, before,** or **after.** It expresses the relationship in time between two different events in the same sentence.

> **Before Sandy left,** she fixed the copy machine.

time expression A phrase that functions as an adverb of time.

> She graduated **three years ago**.
> I'll see them **the day after tomorrow**.

transitive verb A verb that is followed by an object.

> I **read** the book.

uncountable (noncount) noun A common noun that cannot be counted. A noncount noun has no plural form and cannot occur with **a, an,** or a number.

> information   mathematics   weather

verb A word that refers to an action or a state.

> Gina **closed** the window.
> Tim **loves** classical music.

verb phrase A phrase that has a main verb and any objects, adverbs, or dependent clauses that complete the meaning of the verb in the sentence.

> Who **called you**?
> He **walked slowly.**

Appendix IV: Correlation to *Grammar Sense 3*

EFFECTIVE ACADEMIC WRITING 3 THE ESSAY	GRAMMAR SENSE 3
Unit 2 Passives and Modal Passives Using Time Clauses	**Chapter 2** The Past **Chapter 3** Future Forms **Chapter 6** The Past Perfect and the Past Perfect Continuous **Chapter 9** Passive Sentences (Part 1)
Unit 3 Real and Unreal Conditionals	**Chapter 15** Real Conditionals, Unreal Conditionals, and Wishes
Unit 4 Adverbial Clauses Noun Clauses	**Chapter 17** Noun Clauses
Unit 5 Gerunds Infinitives	**Chapter 11** Contrasting Gerunds and Infinitives
Unit 6 Restrictive and Nonrestrictive Clauses	**Chapter 13** Relative Clauses with Subject Relative Pronouns **Chapter 14** Relative Clauses with Object Relative Pronouns